Picky Eating Solutions

Bringing the Joy of Real Food Back to the Table

Betsy Hicks

with contributions from
Pediatrician John Hicks, MD

Editor: Susan Geye
Cover Ilustration: Lisa Roseman
Layout and Design: Signalfire

Letters From Parents

Dayna Hebermehl

Mom of two recovered picky eaters

Betsy, thank you so much for writing this book! *Picky Eating Solutions* is such a refreshing but thorough "how-to guide" on ways to incorporate healthy vegetables into my children's meals. I like how you explained the process of how to add nutrition to all meals, even for the pickiest of eaters, and provided a clear glimpse into the metabolic processes that could be a cause of picky eating. A great resource for all parents!

Cheryl Stolarick

It's comforting to know where your journey began and how you got to the place you are today. I guess just knowing that you went through this makes it easier to accept your advice. It was very eye-opening to read about GMO foods and how we turned into a society that relies on pre-packaged foods. You also did a great job explaining how our digestive system works. That has always been very confusing to me.

The way you broke down your ideas for eliminating picky eating by age or sensory difficulties or verbal or nonverbal children was of tremendous help. I also like all your ideas on the different textures. My son David seems to be like Joey and likes only the creamy or crunchy foods.

Going into this, I never thought our kitchen could really be holding us back. This chapter was fantastic for me. I've always used the excuse that I'm not a good cook, but like you said, no one is a good cook when they start. I'm actually going to get a new apron-which will totally motivate me. I'm also going to reorganize our kitchen—it is a disaster! This may take awhile, but I never realized how much this was really holding me back from cooking.

All in all, Betsy you have inspired me in so many different ways. Some of the things you said in the book were really "Ah-Ha" moments for me. This has been a very hard two years for our family, and I don't know how many times I've shut down and felt like I just can't move on. I'm a person who gets very excited and motivated and ready to do a million things at once, and I set myself up for disaster every time. You outlined in your book some different goals and told us to actually write them down and take small steps, and that's the advice I really need to stick to my plan.

I think this book is going to help so many parents out there, who feel overwhelmed like me and just don't know where to start, or are stuck giving in to our child's demands because we just can't stand the screaming any longer. Thank you so much!

Table of Contents

Dedication

To Jessie, Joey, and Mia
Three different children… three different lessons.

Lessons from the Past

I remember a time when I was married to my ex-husband, worked full time, and we did not have children. I would come home from a long commute, fall onto the couch, and watch TV, begging at times to go out to eat because I couldn't manage making dinner. I thought those were tough times.

I got pregnant and had twin babies. I would love them, feed them, and care for them all day and night. They slept a lot. I had those free moments to cook, clean, and dream of the wonderful life my babies would have. I thought those were tough times.

When he was two, my son Joey screamed a lot. Some days he would cuddle, and some days not. He wasn't speaking. He was diagnosed with autism. My mom was diagnosed with terminal cancer; my best friend announced she was moving away. Those times were tough.

My son's autism became severe. He screamed from sun up to sun down. He cried himself to sleep. He banged his head to the point of having bumps line his forehead. He bit himself. He woke up with night terrors. I was pregnant again—throwing up for months—trying to handle my children—not knowing what was ahead. The times were getting tougher.

I had a new baby. My mother died. Joey still screamed most of his waking day. I found out he had about 50 food allergies, and I had no idea how to cook the few things he could eat. My marriage was failing. We were spending every penny we had on treatments for Joey. Life was unimaginably tough.

I meet many families who hear my story and wonder how I made it through each day, but I felt that telling you the progression of my life was poignant. It was not one whopping blow. It was a series of contrasts that led me to invaluable personal growth. I have had many people say to me, "I couldn't have done it." I always say, "Yes, you could, because you have no choice." You have to take it one day at a time and NEVER stop dreaming of what it is you want. Every day I would fall asleep imagining the life I wanted: The child who laughed, the husband who was loving and kind, the house in the woods. All of that came to me.

When you are feeling overwhelmed by your life, write about what it is that you DO want. You don't have to show it to anyone, but savor the feeling of what it feels like to be in that place, with that person, enjoying that lifestyle. You cannot change others. It is not their job to please you—it is your job to please yourself. It feels wonderful to help people you love, and it's good for the soul. But it's not good when your help comes with ulterior motives and strings attached, trying to make people be who you want them to be.

Most importantly, you cannot give if you are empty. I used to get really upset with people who would say to me, "Go relax, get a massage, get your nails done, and take some time for yourself."

"Really?" I would say in anger and frustration, "And who is going to watch that my son doesn't kill himself during that time, and who will nurse my baby, and who is going to start preparing the next meal? Oh, and by the way, should I cancel my son's therapy that week so I can do those things for myself?" I slipped into the martyr role very nicely. In hindsight, I now think Joey would have received far more benefit from having a relaxed mom than from weekly therapy.

As I started to journal about what I wanted, those things naturally began to show up in my life. I was approved for a state grant that paid for me to get home support. I found amazing therapists that came to my home and worked with Joey. I found support and encouragement from parents facing the same diet challenges, and we created meals together. But nothing holds a candle to the fulfillment of my greatest desire; meeting my husband John—a man who loved me beyond compare, and was determined to help me with my son.

I find it funny when I meet someone now who does not know about my past. They might say, "Wow, you are a parent of three teenagers, you run a business, and you teach so many classes, I don't know how you do it." I just laugh. I remember how hard my past really was. I don't revisit those emotions, but remember how it molded and shaped me, and for that I have tremendous appreciation.

Special Thanks...

It is with much appreciation that I thank the following people for their contributions:

Susan Geye, you are so much more than an editor and so much more than a friend. You are the voice of my inner guidance who helped me unfold the words, open my heart, and bring this book to life. Thank you for sharing your talents with me and the world!

Beth Van De Boom, who is the most amazing teacher. My soft-spoken friend gets a voice with this book, and I am so grateful that she has shared so much with both John and me over the years.

My amazing husband, John, who loves me each moment of the day, encourages me with each breath, and lovingly does the dishes.

Mia, who swore to me that she would never eat healthy once she left the house, has turned into a "foodie." Thank you for celebrating your food and appreciating everything I make.

Jessie, who I promise I will never make sunflower burgers for again, thank you for making organic "cool" at your school and for loving sprouts as much as you do.

And finally, Joey, who has been my greatest teacher in this lifetime! Thank you for being picky. Thank you for motivating me. Thank you for having autism. You are a gift!

Preface

I have worked with special needs children and their diets for well over a decade. Prompted by the onset of my son's severe autism in 1995, my world revolved around special menus and food restrictions. I became an expert in extreme creative cooking, to the point where I could have hosted my own Food Network cooking show, "Make a Meal From Nothing!" My son Joey was unable to eat gluten, milk products, corn, soy, peanuts, apples, and bananas… even with a food sensitivity list stretching close to 50 foods, I could take unusual ingredients and create a healthy meal.

Over time, I turned my knowledge and experience into a career as a diet counselor, working with a variety of doctors, and eventually my husband, Dr. John Hicks. My specialty was restrictive diets. In fact, "restriction" in general became my specialty. It seemed like the harder I worked and the more I struggled, the better I felt about my son and my parenting skills.

The truth is, picky eating is a shameful secret for many parents, and a huge source of anxiety, frustration, and helplessness. Even the best-intentioned parents struggle with the hard reality of making changes to their family's eating habits when dealing with a picky eater. In my diet counseling practice, I tried to set up support groups for parents who were all dealing with the same issues. To my shock and amazement, the same people who begged me for help never showed up for group meetings. After some heart to heart conversations with my "no-show" parents, I realized the depth of their embarrassment and guilt over picky eating. They could paste "My Child is an Honor Student" on their bumper, dress their kids in nice clothes, take them to church, and have them say, "Please" and "Thank you," but they couldn't get them to eat a vegetable.

The grandparents were even more frustrated. They called, pleading me to help their adult children understand that they had power and choices when it came to feeding their own kids. In their generation, there were no food options. If food was on the table, you said "Grace," and obediently ate what was in front of you. With no chemicals, additives, or genetic modifications in the food, there were no food cravings, no food-induced tantrums, and no "fast food cooks" behind the kitchen counter making special meals for the picky eater. Parents didn't coddle children the way many do today. I knew that until the parents were ready and determined to change, there was nothing I could do. Repeatedly, I had to explain that if the grandparents tried to force the issue, the parents would resist. Instead, I told them to model healthy eating in their own home, without lectures and blame, and hope that their commitment to health and wellness created the impetus for change.

Two years ago, I set out to write a book on picky eating—a book that would take a tough stand on parents that "allowed" their picky eating children to control the dinner table and their lives. But as I worked on the book, the light slowly dawned—I realized that my strict guidelines and attitude left some parents with even more anxiety and guilt. If I really wanted to help families, my rigid approach had to change.

So, I took a step back and asked myself, "What was this book really about? Is there a perfect formula for teaching picky eaters to love variety? Must every meal be perfectly nutritious? How could I show families the joy and incredible benefit of cooking and eating real food?" Looking back, I remembered how difficult it was to get Joey to eat anything—and how far we had to go before we had peace and peas at the dinner table. I had to accept where parents were in their struggle to deal with picky eating, and come from a place of love and support, not judgment and blame. "Do the best you can" became my new mantra.

And so let us begin this book from a place of acceptance. You are where you are. Leave all judgments and blame behind. I learned that guilt and struggle did not make me a better parent or "cure" Joey's picky eating. Instead, it was love and acceptance of myself as well as my children, which led all of us to successful choices, and a happier dinner table. Whether you are aiming at expanding an already good basic diet, or simply trying to get the first vegetable down your child, feel the excitement of change without pressure of where you are going. Approach this with kindness and love. As of this moment, we're in this together.

Part I:
Introduction to Picky Eating—My Story

My own personal story was my greatest education in the transformational power of healthy eating. My teachers are my three children, my colleagues, countless books, and my clients. But of all the lessons I have learned, none were taught with as much force as those taught by my son Joey. At the age of six months, he developed an extremely severe case of autism, and my world was suddenly turned upside down.

Joey screamed all day long and could not be comforted. His body was in pain, and as I searched for help, traveling from doctor to doctor, no one had answers, only speculations. My marriage, finances, and personal health were completely falling apart. Joey had a twin sister, Mia, who also had developmental delays. I tried to give her as normal of a childhood as possible. But it was often too convenient to ignore her challenges, as Joey monopolized all of my time and energy.

One thing was very clear. Traditional medicine did not have any answers. I was told to institutionalize Joey, as he was without hope and needed to be heavily medicated. That answer never felt right to me. During those terrible times, I was not consumed with a desire to "cure" my son, but rather just have him be well. He was sick, yet my pediatrician at the time would tell me, "That's just the autism." I remember thinking how absurd that was. On the one hand, the medical community was convinced that autism had no biomedical connections, yet they readily accepted that these children lived in pain. Autism I could live with; suffering I couldn't.

When Joey was four years old, I discovered that certain foods triggered his behavior—gluten, casein (milk protein), eggs, corn, and the list went on and on. There were more foods Joey couldn't tolerate then foods he could actually eat.

In fact, Joey ate only one thing: Barbara's Brown Rice Crisp cereal and rice milk. No disrespect to Barbara, but that was a terrible diet. However, he simply wouldn't eat anything else! People would ask me, "Can't you get him to eat anything but cereal?" Hearing that question would tear me apart inside. Raised with a strong Italian heritage, I lived for feeding my children. I felt like a failure as a mother, but I didn't have the understanding of nutrition to motivate me. As I started to listen to alternative practitioners and read every ounce of information I could find, I began to learn about ingredients that I could use to form foods my son would eat.

I became a kitchen slave in order to find food that I could feed my son. At the time, there were very few cookbooks on allergen free foods and the Internet was in its infancy. I kicked in every ounce of creativity I had. By this time, my daughter Jessie had been born. I woke up at 5:00 a.m. every morning, and headed for the kitchen before the three children would demand my time. I created some pretty unusual concoctions, but my son finally started to experiment and have success with different foods.

It was in that pre-dawn kitchen where I started playing with textures. Joey only ate two: crunchy and smooth. Everything I made followed these two textures, and Joey's diet looked like this:

Breakfast

- Creamed buckwheat, cooked whole amaranth, or rice cereals (smooth)
- Fried sweet potatoes (crunchy)
- Turkey sausage fried in oil (crunchy)
- Dehydrated dried fruit (crunchy)

Lunch

- Homemade chicken nuggets (crunchy on the outside, but with smooth pureed chicken inside)
- Pureed vegetable soup (smooth, and I would switch vegetables so that he got a variety of nutrients)
- Tapioca flour and coconut milk crackers (crunchy—these were his favorite foods. I would alternate adding chopped nuts and vegetables to the cracker recipe to create a crunchy texture)

Dinner

- Meat pounded very thin, and than breaded (crunchy)
- Vegetables pureed with olive oil (Smooth—he was sensitive to Ghee at the time, but that would have been an even better fat)

Special Occasions

- Homemade potato French fries (crunchy)

Joey was still having misdiagnosed pain, but it was far less severe than when I began experimenting with a special diet. It was wonderful to see color in his cheeks again, and to see him finally show signs of growth, where there had been none for years. In an effort to help other parents who were struggling for answers like I was, I started a nutrition support group both online, and at a local health foods store. I was a sponge for any information I could get, and any tips that could improve the life of my son.

In September of 2000, I met my now husband, Dr. John Hicks, at an autism conference. By that time, I was an expert on "special diets." I had written a small recipe book, organized more support groups, and was a part-time diet counselor for area doctors. John told me that over 40% of the children in his practice were on the autism spectrum, and many of them were picky eaters. When he learned of my background, he asked me to work in his office, and my career took off. A year later, so did our relationship.

Once we were together, John and I started Pathways Medical in Delavan, Wisconsin, and eventually changed the name to

Elementals Living. The clinic originally opened to treat children with autism, but soon expanded into an adult and child holistic health center. Nutritional support and healthy eating formed the foundation of our work at the clinic and in our family kitchen at home. I have now worked with thousands of parents over the years and each one has a story that teaches me new methods for helping all our children enjoy healthy food.

My children are now in middle school and high school. They have traveled the nutritional highway from Velveeta to spinach and beyond, and are now educated and enthusiastic eaters. They don't have perfect diets, nor do I expect them to, but their overall understanding of nutrition will feed them well for a lifetime. My daughters, who balked at my nutritious ways for years, make some really great food and beverage choices now, even when I'm not looking over their shoulder!

For those of you who are struggling with picky eating and food-related issues, I know how hard it can be to make changes. The true facts of nutrition aren't taught in school—and many kids today have no idea what a home-cooked meal made with real food really tastes like.

My passion is to help families like yours learn to understand and appreciate the importance and joy of real food—food that not only tastes good, but that is good for you! *Picky Eating Solutions* will introduce you to important nutrition basics and information about how the body uses food. For instance, how many people really know how their digestive system works? Once you understand nutrition basics, and what your children need in order to stay healthy, you'll learn why picky eating can occur, and what you can do to overcome it.

Many parents live in shame and guilt over what they feed their children. Others are simply ignorant of the dangers of malnutrition on a growing body and brain. It's easy to lose sight of the importance of a good meal when you are constantly on the run, juggling a busy life, and multiple schedules. You may think that it costs too much to buy organic food. Or that it takes too long to shop and prepare "real meals" for dinner. With two working parents, and three busy teen-agers, we have a hectic family life, but we make time for nutritious and delicious meals that everyone enjoys.

I wrote this book based on my personal experience and the experience of countless parents just like you. You can take back control of your dinner table and your kitchen! Yes, it does take persistence and consistency. No, you don't have to incorporate all of the techniques and strategies at once. Go at a pace that works for you. We can control what we feed to our children. We can teach them the value and joy of good food. And we can take comfort in knowing that the good food they eat is their best foundation for a healthy future.

What is a Picky Eater?

There is no official definition of a picky eater. The general consensus is that if your child eats a very limited diet, avoids a large number of foods, or even whole classes of foods (especially vegetables), has an aversion to trying new foods that are unfamiliar, and has strong food preferences, including preparation methods and presentation, then your child probably qualifies as a picky eater.

Often the first time a parent hears the term "picky eater" regarding their own child, it is from someone outside the family. You may hear, "Wow! Your child is really fussy! Are chicken nuggets and fries all he/she eats?" from a friend, relative, or even the regular waiter at your favorite restaurant. For most kids, there is no defining moment when they turn into a "picky eater." Maybe your child was an amazing eater as a toddler, but somewhere along the way, you found yourself making separate dinners, and now it's "normal" to accommodate every special request morning, noon, and night. Or maybe your child struggled to eat right from the start—slow to adapt to solids, with difficulty chewing and swallowing food. Some kids, especially as they get older, seem to relish the "food fights" at the dinner table, leaving you exhausted and frustrated, and leaving the vegetables and healthy food on the half-finished plate. If you recognize yourself in any of these scenarios, or suspect that there may be a problem, then you bought the right book, and help is at hand.

My intention for this book is to support you and your child. I care about peace in the home as much as I care about the nutrition your child needs, but my experience has taught me that letting your child eat whatever and whenever he/she wants does not promote long-term peace. Life is full of adventure and variety—and chronic picky eating keeps everyone from the full enjoyment and experience of a lifetime of happy and healthy eating. If your current system works for you, then keep going. I'm not here to point fingers, but rather to help you find ways to support your best instincts. You have better intuition about your child than anyone ever could. However, if you picked up this book because you are intrigued, or feel like you could be doing more, then there is a part of you that is not resonating with your child's diet. So let's work together!

Just as there is no definition of picky eating, there is no agreement on how it happens. Your child's learned behavior, cultural and family influences, physical traits, emotional make-up—even hereditary links play a role in creating a picky eater. Some research suggests that one of the strongest indicators is a parent who was also a picky eater as a child. [1] Regardless of how it happens, a picky eater can gradually take over the kitchen and your life. Many of you will recognize this scenario:

"I really don't mind making each child something different from the main dinner that the rest of us are having each night. They need to eat something!"

I urge you to find another hobby. Of course, if a child has food allergies or intolerances, then making a separate dinner is understandable, but most of us do it out of guilt or to avoid a fight. My excuse was guilt. I grew up during a time when guilt was a virtue, constantly felt that I was not good enough, and it was "my fault" for just about everything that happened. When I became a parent, I coddled my children to the point of exhaustion. Don't get me wrong—I certainly agree that occasionally making a child's favorite meal or treat is a wonderful thing to do. But you are doing a large disservice to your child, to your family, and to yourself, to always make the "favorite food" no matter what everyone else is eating. Contrast and variety at the table, and in life, is a wonderful thing. I would probably eat sushi every night, as I dearly love it. But if I only get it twice a month, I enjoy it so much more, not to mention all the other wonderful food that I would miss if I ate sushi every single night! You don't wear the same clothes day after day, so why would you want to eat the same thing over and over? How fun to travel to different countries, try new restaurants, and know that different flavors and food experiences abound, and that eating a variety of good food is an easy way to optimize your nutritional health.

"As long as he's growing, my doctor told me not to worry about my son's picky eating."

The medical community downplays the problem of picky eating, chalking it up to toddlers' claims to independence, a decrease in appetite as growth rates slow down, and "normal" finicky eating behavior. How many parents have heard their pediatrician say, "Relax. It's just a phase they go through." When it comes to eating vegetables, more often than not, they also tell parents that, "Most kids don't like vegetables," and they say that's typical, too!

The doctors are right—it's not only typical, it's an epidemic, but it certainly isn't "normal." The question is, "Why aren't people doing something about it?" In comparison, based on rates from 2004-2006, nearly 40% of people will get some form of cancer in their lifetime. [2] No one would think to shrug his or her shoulders, and say, "Don't worry—cancer is 'normal!'"

Most pediatricians receive little nutritional training in medical school. They are woefully ignorant of the power of food to impact health—many of them have health issues of their own that could be cured through nutritional support and a truly healthy diet. Think outside the mainstream box… and don't accept picky eating as "normal!"

"If I take away his favorite crackers and cereal, he'll starve."

Does this sound familiar? If your child is only eating French fries, crackers, cereal, and bottled juice; here's the sad truth: Your child is already starving. He may be getting calories, but all of those foods are almost completely void of nutrition. Also, none of those foods even existed 100 years ago. Did parents worry that their children would "starve" because they wouldn't eat the chicken and vegetables on the dinner table? Kids were happy to eat, even if they didn't "love" everything on their plate. They didn't snack all day long. They got daily exercise, and they didn't have "flavor enhanced" foods to tempt them away from eating healthy real food.

"It's not worth the fight to get them to eat healthy foods."

Then don't make it a fight. Make it a rule. It takes two people to "fight"—don't argue back and engage in a power struggle. Ultimately, you're in charge, aren't you? A child won't die from a tantrum. A child won't die from going to bed hungry for one night. But a childhood spent eating fake food, not getting proper nutrition, and throwing the body systems off balance with toxic preservatives and artificial flavors can set a child up for autoimmune disease, diabetes, and worse.

"But our schedule is so tight, I don't have time to cook."

Would you say, "But my schedule doesn't allow me to give my child the medicine he needs to stay alive three times EACH day?" Fortunately, it's not quite that dire, but it IS a matter of priorities. We all have choices. The constant sports and extra-curricular activities make it increasingly difficult for families to have a meal together.

If it's working late that makes it hard for you, then find the time in your schedule to enjoy a family meal… it doesn't have to be dinner. You need to find your own balance and own routine. There are plenty of nutritious choices that are quick to assemble and eat. Healthy eating should not take a back seat to the frenetic pace of family life. When home schedules are exceptionally tight, try just making one meal a priority. In my home, I don't mind the quick breakfasts and school lunches as much when dinner is filled with organic meats and vegetables.

The Origins of Modern Food Culture in America

Let me take you back one hundred years, to a time when food was enjoyed, appreciated, and accepted in whatever form it was served. The food everyone ate was pure, simple, and naturally nutritious. Fixing a separate meal for children was unheard of—kids gratefully ate what was put in front of them. (And if they didn't like something, they ate it anyway.) There were no juice boxes, Goldfish crackers, Happy Meals, special dinners for picky eaters, or "children's menus" in restaurants. What happened?

The history of food in America is a complex and fascinating story, and way beyond the scope of this book. The following quick summary, based on the website below, helps explain how Americans went from the farm table to the fast food table in the last 100 years. If you would like to learn more, go to www.foodtimeline.org.

When the industrial revolution came, it ushered in a revolution in food as well. Local farming methods and harvesting techniques fell victim to the mechanized and centralized processing technology used in modern factories. At the same time, as more and more women entered the workforce, they didn't have time to "slave away" over dinner—and the new convenience products that the big food companies were developing meant freedom from cooking home made meals.

World War II was a pivotal turning point in the kitchen, waging war on home-cooked meals "made from scratch." The food industry created mass-produced canned, ready-made, and freeze-dried meals to feed the troops in the field. With increased demands on women's time, food companies and advertisers seized the opportunity to promote their packaged, processed, and preserved food as superior to home cooking. Frozen TV dinners, cake mixes, Jell-O, Tang, artificial colors, flavors, and chemical additives replaced fresh food at the table. The media portrayed mothers that embraced the new food technology as smart and savvy—no longer "slaves" to the hot stove.

Fast food dealt another blow to people's healthy relationship to food. Although White Castle opened their first outlet in 1921, it was the meteoric rise of McDonalds in the 1950's, [3] combined with the rise of suburbs, a super-highway system, and the wide-spread availability of the automobile that turned the American family dinner into an "eat-on-the-run" processed, preserved, additive-filled, and pre-packaged nutritional time bomb. In 2004, about half of total food expenditures came from the "away from home market," up from 34 percent in 1974. [4] Sadly, we have evolved into a society addicted to refined sugar and carbohydrates, bad fat, empty calories, chemical additives, and enhanced and artificial flavors. Back in the 1950's, there were 2,000 pre-packaged food items in stores, a drop in the bucket compared to the 60,000 pre-packaged food items available in super Wal-Marts, Targets, and grocery stores today. [5] How many thousands are snack and convenience products aimed at kids? It's no surprise that food manufacturers spent $7 billion in advertising in 1997, 22% focused on prepackaged and processed convenience foods. [6] McDonalds spends $1.4 billion a year in advertising their fast food experience. [7] And where are the ad dollars going? Seventy-five percent went to television ads—and fast food restaurants spent over 95% of their ad budgets on TV advertising. [8] It's no wonder that childhood obesity rates are soaring, and Type 2 Diabetes is now a disease of the young. Kids struggle with food allergies that were unheard of a decade ago. The stark truth is that the billion dollar-plus processed food industry is drugging our children with processed food, and making our job as parents more challenging. Misleading media advice and an uneducated medical community compound and confuse the problem.

Our culture, values, and lifestyle are reflected in what we eat and drink. Soft drinks, fast foods, giant portions at chain restaurants, packaged and processed foods, and an obsession with snacks—these are the societal markers that define mainstream American food culture.

But the tide is slowly turning. Prompted by wonderful educational organizations such as Weston A Price (www.westonaprice.org) and Slow Food (www.slowfood.com), and the rise of organic farming and local-source foods, we are waking up to the fact that the majority of what is in our grocery stores, and in our children's bodies is poison, and that we have a choice to do things differently.

We can't put the blame solely on the food industry's plate. Many parents have lost control of their own kitchen. I have been a pediatric diet counselor for over a decade under the guidance of my husband, a pediatrician. Every day I see the medical catastrophes caused by an unhealthy diet and picky eating. Additionally, I feel the frustration of parents who have "tried everything," because I was that parent. Luckily, there is another way. Through education and support, determination and persistence, parents who understand the power of real food give their children a precious gift—a healthy foundation for life.

Reasons for Picky Eating

It begins with bags of Cheerios, Gold Fish crackers, and toddler marketed "finger food" in special fun packaging. Tupperware even makes little containers for "parents on the go" to keep a stash of snacks whenever peace is needed. No one fell into this trap as much as I did. I was constantly feeding my children and then wondering why they wouldn't eat a meal. They quickly became little carb addicts. With my strong "food = love" heritage, my children were never allowed to be hungry. That's really sad when you think about it—because healthy hunger and anticipation is a wonderful prelude to enjoying good food. Isn't a meal gratifying when you are hungry?

During a visit with my niece and her young toddler Ronan, we went to the park. Nearly every child there had easy access to some form of a simple carb snack. Little Ronan naturally went up with curiosity and hunger to the rows of tempting snacks. His mom quickly turned him away and distracted him. "We're going to dinner after the park and you can eat there," she calmly stated. Floored, and proud of her lesson, I wondered why I never thought of doing that when my children were small! Like so many well-meaning mothers, I thought that if I didn't feed my children all the time, I was a "bad mother," and they would think I didn't love them.

When we arrived at the restaurant, the well-meaning server brought over a few crackers for Ronan to eat, but his mom did not accept them, letting her son wait with the other diners to get his meal. Ronan ate mounds of vegetables and meat and showed very little interest in the carbs. A children's menu was nowhere to be found at our table!

Now, in no way am I suggesting that you withhold food if your children are truly hungry. Although it is true that little growing bodies need to eat more often, as they burn so much energy, three meals and two snacks each day are ample. And always offer water—water should always be the drink of choice for thirsty little bodies.

Biomedical Considerations for Picky Eaters

A biomedical evaluation is an important first step when evaluating a potential picky eater. In some cases, there are physiological problems that impact a child's ability to taste, smell, chew, swallow, and process food. The taste bud itself is incredibly complicated. The tongue has between 2,000—8,000 taste buds, with enormous variability in where the buds are distributed on the tongue, and the varying amounts of the different receptor cells. Taste buds are composed of 50—150 taste receptor cells that are bundled together in clusters. [9] The taste receptor cells can identify sweet, salty, sour, bitter, as well as the strong taste of aged cheese or meats, a taste called Umami. An imbalance in the taste bud receptor types may make certain foods more or less appealing. If there is variability in the number of taste buds, in the sensitivity, or distribution, any of these can effect picky eating, however, the instance of this is relatively rare.

Another contribution to taste is smell. Seventy to seventy-five percent of what we perceive as taste actually comes from our sense of smell. Smell receptors are incredibly sensitive and are found at the top of the nasal cavity, beneath the brain, and behind the bridge of the nose. The sense of smell is greatly variable. The sensitivity may be so acute that levels of odor that are not perceptible to most people may be strongly perceived by some children and adults. The olfactory system is very sensitive to viruses, toxins, and heavy metals. Some children are very sensitive to heat and cold, and may have issues with foods that are outside their tolerance range.

Smell and taste belong to our chemical sensing system (chemosensation). Taste receptor cells and olfactory cells transmit messages via neurons to the brain, where specific smells or tastes are identified. A neuron malfunction in the transmission of the signals to the brain for processing can affect how food feels, smells, and tastes.

The neurons can be affected by amino acid deficiencies, ion abnormalities, cell membrane abnormalities, blockage of impulse transmission, and cellular energy. Diagnosis of the problem requires a detailed understanding of the neurotransmitter system, and what to do to correct the problem. That goes well beyond the scope of this book. My husband, Dr. John Hicks, can detect imbalances and restore the balance and functionality of the neurons.

What is important to know is that all neurons depend on cellular energy for their functions. The cellular energy cycle requires minerals, iron, B vitamins, CQ10-(a naturally occurring enzyme that supports healthy cell development), glutathione-(plays an important role in the de-tox system), and NADPH and FADH-(electron-donating molecules that play an important role in metabolism), and is susceptible to heavy metal toxicity from aluminum, fluoride, mercury, cadmium, arsenic, and antimony. If there are variances in the levels of sodium, potassium, calcium, or magnesium, these ions will affect the neuron transmission. If there are abnormalities in the synaptic junctions, this can also affect transmission. We will explore this subject in more detail in Part II of the book.

The complex interaction of sensory and muscular systems can create many issues that could affect picky eating. These may be from toxins that affect the sensory system itself, or the neuromuscular system. The issues can be with the tongue, its motion, inefficient chewing, mishandling of food within the mouth, or the lip, tongue, and cheek activity. It could be further related to esophageal motility or irritation of the esophageal tissues. It could also be related to possible reflux. The other contributors to potential issues with picky eating can be difficulty in physically handling the food in the mouth, or the process of chewing and swallowing. This book was not written to address the more complex biomedical reasons for picky eating. If you suspect that your child may have any physical issue that could affect his/her ability to eat, please see the appropriate medical personnel. There are many speech and sensory integration therapists that specialize in picky eating biomedical disorders. Be sure and research their experience and philosophy of care, and remember that as a parent, you know your child best!

Are You or Your Child a Picky Eater? Take the Picky Eating Test

There is no scoring for this test. You will not be rated, or judged. I simply include the tests here because it helps with the awareness that your eating habits, or those of your child's, are possibly keeping you and your family from the freedom to experience the incredible variety of foods that are available to sample and enjoy. As one 12 year-old girl put it, "I don't like being a picky eater because it makes people sad and mad." If picky eating is keeping you from traveling, trying new restaurants or cuisines, eating at a friend's house, going to Grandma's, or feeling confident that you can always find something to eat, than maybe it's time to take a look at your diet and give yourself permission to make some changes. The other reason to change is nutrition—we all want our children to be healthy, and what they eat today is what their health will be tomorrow. This book can help you determine what you want—for you and your children—and show you the best way for you to achieve your goals.

For Children

- Does your child have to have the "exact" brand of favorite foods—like crackers or pizza or chicken nuggets, or whatever the favorite foods are—because he/she will only eat one kind?
- Would your child rather not eat than have to eat something new?
- Do you fix special meals for your child to ensure that he/she gets "something" to eat?
- Does your child have problems with texture?
- Are you bored with the options your child is willing to eat?
- Is it a struggle to find something that your child will eat on just about any menu in most restaurants?
- Do you ever feel anxiety when going out to eat because you are unsure if your child can find anything that he/she will eat?
- Do you find yourself eating at the same restaurants to avoid surprises or confrontations?
- Do you feel anxiety when going to someone's house for dinner because your child will not like what is being served, and do you sometimes bring something from home to eat for your child as a result?
- When you travel in the United States, do you need to restrict your food choices to chain restaurants where you already know the menu?
- Are you afraid to travel internationally because the unfamiliar foods might be a problem for your child to eat?

For Adults

- Were you afraid to try new foods when you were a child?
- Did you dislike vegetables as a child?
- Do you dislike vegetables now?
- Do you have strong cravings for certain foods? Which ones?
- Do you ever feel addicted to your favorite foods—that you "have to have" your afternoon diet drink, donut, or French fries?
- Is it a challenge to find something you like on just about any menu in most restaurants?
- Do you ever feel anxiety when going out to eat because you are unsure of the exact way something is prepared?
- Do you find yourself eating at the same restaurants to avoid surprises?
- Do you feel anxiety going to someone's house for dinner because you are not sure you will like what is served?
- When you travel in the United States, do you need to restrict your food choices to chain restaurants where you already know the menu?
- Are you afraid to travel internationally because of the unfamiliar foods you may have to eat?

Part II: The Relationship Between Food, the Body, and Picky Eating

Overview

As parents, we think we know our kids inside and out—from freckles, to birthmarks, to the way their hair curls on the nape of their neck—the landscape of their bodies is near and dear. But do you know what goes on inside that little (or not so little) body when it comes to the food they eat?

Truthfully, most of us don't have a clue how our body converts food into the energy it needs to sustain life. Where does that chicken nugget go? Why do Skittles turn some children from docile to dangerous? What happens if kids only eat a limited diet? Why would my doctor say I shouldn't worry when my son isn't growing? From the digestive system to brain function to detoxification, I find it amazing that most people know so little about their bodies and how they work. What your child eats on a daily basis is the most important ingredient in a recipe for a long and healthy life. It also plays a huge role in picky eating.

Nutrition is the broad term that describes what the body needs in order to stay alive. Nutrition comes from the food we eat. Or does it? Years ago, I set out to write a book on food and nutrition, but quickly scrapped the idea. At the time, the subject was controversial, and even my own opinions were changing dramatically from year to year. Now, after 15 years of studying food through cooking and the nutritional needs of children, coupled with my husband's 35 years of pediatric and biomedical experience, I feel qualified to gently guide you in this area. Why do I use the term gently? Because there is no ONE WAY to eat well for a lifetime. This book is not intended to "scare you" into making changes in your kitchen and on your table as the only way to cure picky eating. I will give you both nutritional and medical guidelines for feeding your children, but the most important ingredient is YOUR confidence and intuition. What feels right to you? Once you understand the basics of good nutrition and how the body uses food, you are empowered to make good decisions for you and your family. Love what you eat, and teach your children to do the same! Eating with joy and gratitude is one of the most important ingredients for a lifetime of healthful eating.

Every year my family has a tradition of picking apples at a nearby orchard, and then eating pulled pork sandwiches with "build your own" caramel apples. There is not one part of me that feels guilty as they are pouring on that caramel and adding sprinkles to the top.

It's a truly special event, and the food is part of the enjoyment. On the other hand, when I see my kids bring home a giant bag of candy after staying at a friend's house, I admit that visions of cavities, yeast overgrowth, and compromised immune systems dance in my head. The bottom line is that education and awareness give all of us the power and confidence to make the right choices for long-term health and wellness. Nothing is more important than that!

This section will help you set the parameters of your child's diet. From my practice, I learned that most parents are completely misinformed about the basics of good nutrition and a healthy diet. The mass production of processed, preserved, modified, and pre-packaged food in the United States has strongly contributed to the increase of diabetes, celiac disease, immune disorders, and developmental disabilities, not to mention the rise in picky eating! Our wealthy country is an embarrassment compared to the nutritional standards of even some developing countries. Our food is chemically preserved in order to last decades on the shelf. Our vegetables grow in nutrient depleted soil, and our chickens are treated with arsenic. Walk the aisles of a standard grocery store, drive the streets to see the abundance of fast food restaurants, and witness our children's school cafeterias and you can't help but wonder what happened to our relationship with food.

During a recent lecture I gave at a high school health class, a student volunteered to let me critique his lunch. His friends assured me that he brought the same thing to eat every day: A can of Mountain Dew, Starburst Gummies, and a pudding cup. His reply,

"I can eat whatever I want as long as I exercise" only added to my concern and slight hysteria. Another student commented that as long as he wasn't fat, why was his diet a problem? The problem is the nutritional foundation of his body is built on chemicals and free radicals—a perfect set up for chronic illness and rapid aging. The basics of nutrition that are taught in most schools are archaic, so it's no wonder that the students had no idea of the damage they were doing to their growing bodies and brains.

Attitudes of apathy and ignorance about nutrition are enhanced by a lack of truthful information from the Food and Drug Administration. The updated Food Pyramid is better than the original, but the government diet standards and even doctor's growth charts do not reflect the true nutritional needs of children and adults. Conflicting advice from medical professionals, mass media, giant food conglomerates, and advertising campaigns just make it more confusing for parents trying to make the right decisions for their children.

Nutrition Basics: What Every Parent Should Know

Nutrition is a vital role in overall health, yet there is so much conflict on what "experts" say is good for you and your child. In all of my studies of nutrition, I have never found one method or diet that I completely agree with, however, there are certain foods that hold dense nutritional value and should be incorporated into your family diet as much as possible.

Throughout this book you will find my suggestions for nutritional "do's" and "don'ts", but many of my clients found it helpful to gradually shift their family towards eating a healthy diet by following a plan. The guidelines listed below may help you prioritize your goals with steps that you feel ready to tackle. Some of you may take on a new step each week, and others will feel more comfortable with a new step each month. Set some goals with your family, and do your best to follow through no matter how quickly you choose to make these changes. The important thing is to commit to long-term change and not get discouraged or quit.

Healthy Eating Plan

1) Begin with adding more water into your diet. If you are a soda, juice, or coffee drinker, drink one glass of water for each soda, juice, or coffee you drink. (To determine how much water you should drink each day, take your weight, divide by two, and that number is how many ounces of water you should drink.)
2) Eat two serving of vegetables each day (not counting corn or potato).
3) Eat some form of protein three times each day.
4) Remove artificial colors from your diet.
5) Remove High-Fructose Corn Syrup (HFCS) from your diet.
6) Remove artificial sweeteners and ingredients that contain excitotoxins.
7) Increase fiber in your diet through fruits, vegetables, and whole grains.
8) Switch to organic protein sources like organic pasture raised chicken, free range organic eggs, grass fed organic beef, and organic nuts, seeds, and beans.
9) Substitute organic dairy products wherever possible.
10) Use as many organic vegetables as possible. Frozen or even canned organic vegetables work well if fresh vegetables are not in season.

The following nutrition chart shows my top choices for each food category to help you choose the healthiest options for your family.

For those of you who want to explore healthy eating and nutrition in more detail, I highly recommend the book, *the world's healthiest foods* by George Mateljan, founder of Healthy Valley Foods. Over 800 pages, it is an incredible collection of the healthiest foods on the planet, with recipes, nutrient listings, explanations of the health benefits of each food, cooking suggestions, eating plans, and diets.

Nutrition Chart		
Vegetables	**Fruits**	**Nuts & Seeds**
Asparagus	Apples	Almonds
Beets	Apricots	Brazil Nuts
Carrots	Avocados	Cashews
Celery, Fennel	Bananas	Chia
Cruciferous Vegetables - Broccoli, Brussel Sprouts, Cauliflower, Cabbage, Bok Choy	Berries - Strawberries, Raspberries, Elderberries, Blueberries, Cranberries, Acai	Flaxseed
Garlic, Onions	Citrus - Lemons, Limes, Grapefruit, Oranges	Hazelnuts
Green Beans	Coconut	Hemp
Green Leafy Vegetables - Spinach, Collard Greens, Kale, Swiss Chard, Arugula, Mustard Greens	Grapes (the darker the better)	Hickory Nuts
Green Peas	Kiwi Fruit	Macadamia Nuts
Mushrooms - Crimini & Shiitake	Melons - Watermelon, Cantaloupe	Pecans
Peppers	Papaya	Poppy Seeds
Potatoes - Red, Purple, and Sweet	Pears	Pumpkin Seeds
Romaine Lettuce	Pineapple	Sesame Seeds
Sea Vegetables - Varieties of Kelp	Plums	Sunflower Seeds
Squash	Tomatoes	Walnuts

Nutrition Chart

Fish & Shellfish	Poultry, Meat, & Eggs	Beans & Legumes
Alaskan & Black Cod	Buffalo	Black Beans
Alaskan Halibut	Chicken - Pasture Raised	Black Eyed Peas
Albacore Tuna	Duck	Garbanzo
Clams	Eggs - Chicken, Duck, Quail, Goose	Kidney Beans
Escargot	Grass Fed Beef	Lentils
Scallops	Lamb - Grass Fed	Lima Beans
Shrimp	Liver	Peanuts
Wild Pacific Salmon	Ostrich	Pinto Beans
	Turkey - Pasture Raised	Red Beans, Adzuki
	Venison	Split Peas

Whole Grains	Herbs	Spices
Amaranth*	Basil	Black Pepper
Buckwheat*	Cilantro	Cardamom
Kamut	Dill	Cayenne & Red Chili Peppers
Millet*	Lemongrass	Cinnamon
Oats*	Mint	Clove
Quinoa*	Mustard Seeds	Cumin
Rice* - Brown, Wild, & Basmati	Oregano	Ginger
Rye	Parsley	Nutmeg
Spelt	Rosemary	Sea Salt
Whole Wheat	Thyme	Turmeric
*These are labeled as gluten-free although some (especially oats) can be contaminated with gluten		

Cooking Oils		
Avocado	Grape Seed & Olive Oil - Cold filtered, expeller pressed	Sesame
Butter	Palm Oil	Sunflower/Safflower - Cold filtered, expeller pressed
Coconut		Walnut (best if not heated)
Ghee		

Picky Eating and the Medical Community

Commentary by John Hicks, MD

When it comes to growth, development, and nutrition for children, the focus of medicine relies on charts standardized in the 1950's, and as long as a child falls in the range from the 5th to the 95th percentile, the medical community acts as if they are growing normally. In residency, we were educated about electrolyte balance, pH balance, and sugar utilization. For extreme malnutrition, we were taught about hyper alimentation (liquid nutrients given intravenously), which was used for premature babies and people in intensive care who were not eating for extensive periods of time. The focus was again, on electrolytes, glucose, basic amino acids, and medium chain triglycerides. There was some information given on basic vitamins, however the teaching was that synthetic vitamins were identical to those vitamins from foods. Pediatricians were also traditionally taught that vitamins are not essential because so many foods like breads and cereals are "enriched and fortified." There was no acknowledgement or discussion of the various food groups, true vitamin complexes, absorbability, and the function of the sub-units of the vitamin complexes. The synthetic vitamins are not the same quality and do not perform the same functions as real food or pharmaceutical grade vitamins. We were given some information on the food pyramid; however, there really wasn't any substantive discussion of nutrition content in foods. The assumption in the standard medical community is that the American diet is adequate and there is really no difference between organic and non-organic foods.

Nutrition is not something that most physicians know about. They were not trained in it, and unless they have sought education beyond medical school training, they are not aware of the use of digestive enzymes, the multiple causes of reflux, the impact of deficient or below normal gut flora (bacteria), and the potential invasive and destructive capacity of what traditional practitioners consider to be low grade bacteria present in the GI tract. There is some discussion of food allergies in IgE form and the possibility of anaphylactic reactions from nuts and shellfish. The focus that does get directed to these issues is about learning specific pathogens and then their specific antibiotic treatments. No real discussion has opened the door to the understanding that not only are the antibiotics killing the bad bacteria, but they are also killing the good bacteria that we need for normal growth and development. From further personal research, the existence of excitoxins, neuropeptides, and food hypersensitivities has shown me that there is a lot more to be considered than just food allergies when looking at the subject of food and nutrition in general and how it affects picky eating.

Excitotoxins are chemicals or amino acids found in MSG, Aspartame, and other artificial ingredients that disrupt neurotransmitters and neuropeptides, and affect brain function—focus, concentration, memory—and they modify our interpretation of taste, which can significantly impact a picky eater. Since neuropeptides effect opioid receptors and therefore modify the ability to perceive pain and the ability to connect to one's physical surroundings, excitotoxins can also impact normal eating-related behaviors of already sensitized children.

Food hypersensitivities do not present the symptoms of food allergies, however, their impact can be on any system in the body, stemming from gastro-intestinal dysfunction to immune hyperactivity. Food hypersensitivities can be leading causes of constipation, diarrhea, irritable bowel, chronic abdominal pain, and enuresis (bed-wetting). When food hypersensitivities are present, there is typically an immune shift, which predisposes the child to autoimmune disease. Therefore, it is imperative that the food hypersensitivities and the immune dysfunctions be addressed, especially if a child is a picky eater.

To find these types of problems you have to be suspicious, because there are no outward physical symptoms when they first start to manifest. Traditional medical training is based on treating the physical symptoms, and a lot of the underlining root issues with many growth and development concerns have no outward physical presentation in the early stages, making them difficult to diagnose.

The reality in medicine today is that there are broad ranges, which are considered to be normal. Doctors are not looking for optimal health. Medicine is focused on finding abnormal values that are out of the acceptable range, not realizing that in metabolic individuality, each person has their optimum level of functioning. As long as a child falls on the growth or development charts, doctors feel that he/she is receiving adequate nutrition. As a parent, nutritional education is necessary to aid your child in becoming all that they can be, and to successfully resolve picky eating issues and behaviors. It is through self-empowerment that true preventative health is attained.

How Do I Know What Food is Really Good for My Family?

Walk through the aisles of any major grocery store. Do you know where the produce comes from? Is it safe to eat? Does the meat have antibiotics? What does "natural" really mean? Should you buy low-fat products? There are hundreds of cereals, snacks, and pre-packaged foods to choose from—all making different nutritional claims—how do you choose?

The trick to healthy eating is to eat "real" foods and avoid the "fake" ones. So what do I mean by real? My favorite way of quickly knowing if the food is real is to ask yourself this question, "Did the food exist 100 years ago?" Back then; just about everything was grown locally, and prepared in its whole form. Maybe that's why I love farmer's markets. The colors, the smells, and the heirloom varieties of vegetables—you can feel the connection between the food and the people that grow it and bring it to market. I pick out my vegetables with tremendous love. When I get home, I wash some varieties right away, trim and pull off stems, and repackage them so they will be comfortable in my refrigerator. Everyday I make sure they have plenty, but not too much air. I treat them like the living things they are. It's true—one could accuse me of going a little overboard, but I appreciate the real-ness of fresh produce.

Now I understand that most people do not wish to spend their time as their vegetables' concierge. "Is the temperature in the crisper bin okay for you? Are you being crowded by the broccoli, because I can move you to the next bin if that's more comfortable?" They want to purchase something cheap, convenient, and easily stackable in the refrigerator, pantry, or freezer. Food manufacturers jumped all over this demand, and responded with pre-packaged, standard-sizing convenience foods for everything... foods with a two-year shelf life and a list of ingredients that remind you of high school chemistry class. "But don't worry," we're told—"they're good for you!" How do you know? Because the commercial told you they were delicious and nutritious? Or was it the coupon with the confident looking mother that sold you? Or was it the demanding child tugging on your coat while you rushed through the grocery store on your way home from soccer practice? Stop. Before you pick up that convenient Lunchable package so your kids can eat in the car, ask yourself, "Is this real food that will nourish their bodies?"

Don't get me wrong—there are plenty of good choices in your local grocer's freezer section, and on the grocery shelves. You can find frozen organic fruits and vegetables, gluten-free breads, organic pizzas, canned products, and ready-made organic meals. There are lots of bad choices, too. So how do you tell the difference between real and fake food? Here are some guidelines to help you make the right choices. (Exceptions are given to some salt cured or fermented meats and vegetables.)

Real	Fake
Made with whole ingredients	Made with ingredients that are not a food group or digestible. Don't let the label "100% Natural" trick you. Wood is natural, but you would get sick if you ate it
Needs refrigeration and will decrease in vibrant color and pleasing fragrance each day	Has a longer shelf life than fresh food typically should. Processed meats are treated with many chemicals to keep sausages, hot dogs, and bacon fresh for weeks
Ingredients contain only foods you know and can pronounce	It is very rare that something that is multi-syllabic is good for you. Some preservatives are better than others. When the company lists the source of these preservatives that can be helpful. I find that many companies will list "why" they put it in. Knowing "why" is not going to help it digest any better or be better for your body*
Spices and herbs	MSG-based "Natural Flavoring"
Milk products	Versions of milk that alter its natural form. Examples would be non-dairy creamers, ice milk, fast food shakes, soft serve ice cream
Butter	Margarine
Cold filtered expeller pressed oils- refer to the Nutrition Chart	Vegetable or other oils that became oils through any type of heat processing

*The ingredient book, *Food Additives: A Shopper's Guide to What's Safe & What's Not* by Christine Hoza Farlow, D.C. lists artificial ingredients and explains what they are and what they do to the body.

The standard rebuttal that I hear over and over is, "I don't have time to shop or cook every day," and I completely understand. But here is the good news: you are living in a time where record amounts of organic food manufacturers are rapidly introducing whole food-based products. More expensive, you say? I won't argue with you there, yes, real food often costs more. But that is like dressing in paper towels in the morning and saying, "Real clothes cost more, so I have to settle on a fast and cheap solution." Real food can be a priority, and still allow you to live within a realistic budget. A whole raw organic chicken costs the same as a large bag of nuggets, but you can make three great meals from the tasty and meaty chicken. Organic beans and rice are extremely affordable. Make a habit of utilizing every part of your vegetables by tossing what isn't appealing to you (celery leaves, broccoli stems, wilting spinach) into vegetable soups, or pureeing them into meatloaf. As amazing as it sounds, there are developing countries that eat a healthier diet than American children do!

Another easy way to tell the difference between real food and "fake food" is to do what I call the "Three P's" Test. Is it processed? Is it preserved? Is it packaged? If the food scores "Three-for-Three" then you know it's fake. Our children beg for these fake foods because they are addicting. The chemicals are formulated to make the fake foods taste and look better than their real counterparts—although some of these fake foods have no natural counterpart (thank goodness!). When the truth came out about the hazards and health risks of smoking, Americans responded vigorously. You wouldn't think of giving your children cigarettes! And yet, the abundance of addictive chemicals and toxins in some of these fake foods will also have a serious long term affect on our health—and especially the health of our children.

The best way to visualize the effects of fake food is to think of the body as a filing cabinet full of separate folders. Amino acids go in this folder, calcium goes in that folder, essential fatty acids in another folder, but then in comes a fake or chemically created food and there is no file for it. The body simply doesn't recognize it as a "food" it can use. What does the body do? It shoves the fake food and related toxins that are not processed into the "junk closet"... and in the body, this is usually the fat cell. When that "fat closet" gets filled, the body builds another fat-filled toxic closet and another, which is one reason why obesity and chronic illness rates are soaring in children and teenagers. Giving the body nutritious and toxin-free real food that it can use and easily process provides the best foundation for a lifetime of health and wellness.

Immediate Effects of Fake Food	Result of Eating Fake Food on the Body
The body does not recognize fake food	Poor digestion
Fake food depletes good bacteria	The formation of food intolerances can occur
The body cannot break the fake food down into usable nutrients	Malabsorption of essential nutrients
Fake food has a negative effect on neurotransmitters	Leads to poor focus, concentration, and altered mood
Fake foods can have a negative effect on epigenomes	Altered DNA
Fake food ingredients weaken the immune system	Decreases resistance to viruses and bacteria
Chemicals and toxins in fake food use up free radical scavengers	Lessens the body's ability to heal
Fake food overworks the pancreas	Increases risk of diabetes
Fake food overworks liver and kidneys in the de-tox system	Blocks detoxification
Fake food attacks mitochondria	Can lead to fatigue and low cellular energy
The body gets empty calories	Body accumulates fat mass and toxins

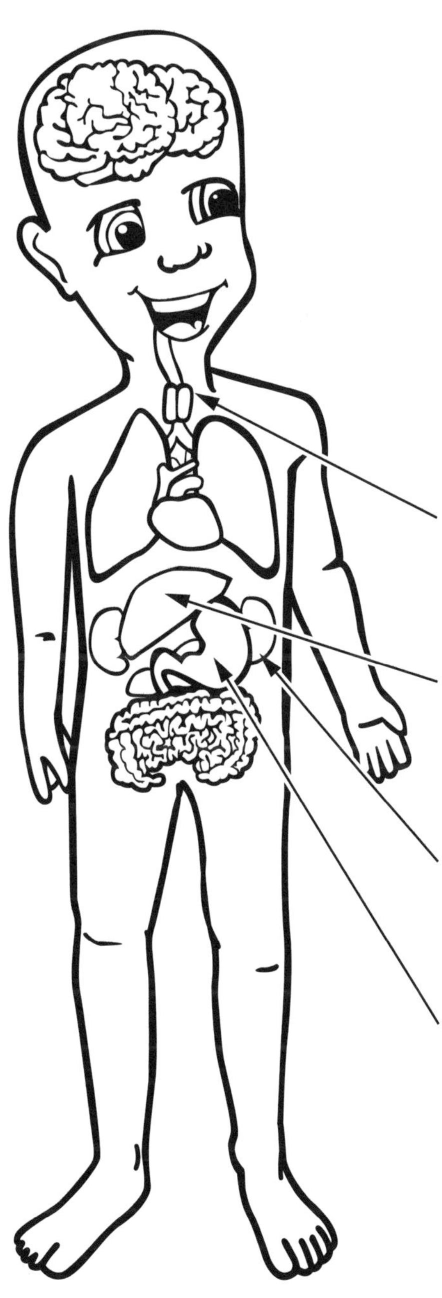

General Health
Decreased energy levels

Brain
Poor focus, concentration, and memory
Altered mood, sleep issues

Ears and Nasal
Respiratory issues, chronic colds, ear and sinus infections

Throat
Sore throats, acid reflux

Thymus
Weakened immune system, decreased resistance to viruses and bacteria, increased allergies

Liver
Decreased ability to eliminate toxins, increased risk of obesity, problems with energy metabolism, digestion, processing and distribution of nutrients

Pancreas
Digestion issues, blood sugar fluctuations and increased risk of diabetes, low cellular energy

Stomach
Poor digestion, acid reflux, and abdominal pain

Intestines
Malabsorption of nutrients, leaky gut, irritable bowel syndrome, constipation, diarrhea, increased risk of Candida

Organic: It's a Matter of Life and Health!

One of the most troubling declines in the food cycle is the "nutritionally dead" soil used to grow the "mega-production" fruits and vegetables available in grocery stores. Modern farming techniques that rob our produce of vitamins, minerals, antioxidants, and probiotics are cheating the well meaning parent that feeds their child a diet rich in meats, vegetables, fruits, and whole grains. If you do not have easy access to organic options, you can supplement your daily diet by purchasing local foods that are in season. Our bodies intuitively dance with the rhythm of the seasons, and eating seasonally supports us in body and spirit.

Washing conventional fruits and vegetables doesn't make them organic, or remove the pesticides! With today's sophisticated production farming methods, the seeds are genetically altered to be "pesticide ready." These are the GMO plants that you'll read more about later. As the crops grow, the pesticides are sprayed on the flower, so that these toxic chemicals actually grow into the produce. Crops are no longer required to rotate, because chemical fertilizers help them grow and be cosmetically appealing. One cannot see a lack of vitamins, although the lack of taste is obvious once you have experienced the organic counterpart. Produce picked while green to allow for transport and shipping time ripens without flavor. It's no surprise that Americans no longer enjoy their vegetables when you realize how far removed they are from the healthy, delicious varieties of a hundred years ago.

The story with meats is even more disheartening because of the inhumane treatment of so many production animals. My great friends, Bob and Beth Van De Boom, own a farm in Wisconsin. I always tease them that their farm is for the cows, sheep, and chickens that suffered in a past life, and now live there as a karmic reward. There is nothing about their farm that makes me feel the least bit sad for these well loved and humanely treated open range animals. You can taste the difference, as they are not fattened up with soy and corn, or routinely given antibiotics, and they live a totally organic life. All of the mass media fears about beef and mad cow disease are unwarranted when you are eating 100% grass fed organic beef. As for chickens, most of the chickens raised in the United States are kept in tiny cages, and fed arsenic to stimulate their appetite so they grow faster to meet production goals. Chickens belong on pastures, eating a variety of food sources to maximize their nutritional value. I challenge any of you to compare the taste of Tyson chicken to the free-range organic chicken that is now readily available in almost any major grocery food store.

The argument that there is not enough land to raise free-range animals is shortsighted. Free-range animals don't require the huge investment in land and equipment that is used to grow the genetically modified corn and soy fed to animals raised with conventional methods. Talk about a dysfunctional food chain! Instead of raising pesticide-laden food for animals or for us, doesn't it make more sense to restore our soil's health, and raise animals the way they used to be raised? When it comes to being "picky eaters," it's time for all of us to demand better tasting food that's better for us!

The good news is that the rise in consumers' environmental and nutritional awareness is leading to a rise in the availability of organic choices, including fresh meat and produce. We can eat healthfully, and it does not need to cost a fortune. Many major food store chains now have a generic line of organic foods. If you compare the price of pizza delivery, packaged foods, soda, and fast food to rice, beans, and seasonal fruits and vegetables that are not prepackaged, and organic cuts of meat that fit your budget, the difference in cost is marginal at best. But the difference in benefits is huge!

One way to control produce costs is to "eat with the seasons." Our bodies are innately programmed to respond to our environment. When it gets cooler out, the body craves warm foods. Everything slows down, and the coolness will slow digestion.

Each season we regenerate different organs that correlate to the foods that ripen during that time. These foods support the function that your body is working to complete.

Foods that are out of season and have to travel long distances to allow you to eat, for instance, strawberries all year long, are picked green and ripened un-naturally. There is an inverse relationship between the length of time it takes for a food to travel from harvest to table and its level of nutrition. The longer it takes—the less nutrition it has. This, in part, is why farmers markets are such a simple way to know what is in season. Although I have seen booths with shipped-in food, most farmers markets feature local farmers selling seasonal foods that are not only easy on your pocketbook, but also so good for your body! It's also a great way to support sustainable agriculture and a healthy seed bank of heirloom fruits and vegetables.

Eating well gives you more energy and vitality, fewer sick days, enhances your physical appearance, improves your overall health, and can often lead to less dependence on medications and medical services. All that, and it tastes better, too!

Food Culprits: Problem Foods for Picky Eaters

A mainstay of too many American diets, these foods can negatively impact the diet, health, and picky eating habits of your children and mine. For those of you who would like to learn more about the manipulation of our food supply, I highly recommend the movie, *Food, Inc.*, a comprehensive documentary on the modern food industry and its impact on our land and our health.

GMO Foods

Genetically modified foods, known as GMO's, are one of the most dangerous and deceptive changes to our food supply, and the giant food corporations that are behind the bio-engineering of our food supply don't want you to know the truth. Genetic modification changes the DNA of the seed organism—generally to make it more pest or disease resistant. In 2003, countries that grew 99% of the global transgenic crops were the United States (63%), Argentina (21%), Canada (6%), Brazil (4%), China (4%), and South Africa (1%) and today the Grocery Manufacturers of America estimate that 75% of all processed foods in the United States contain a GM ingredient. [10] The spin from companies such as Monsanto—one of the giants of the GMO industry—is: “We make it better.” Better? Really? We may be able to grow it faster and cheaper, but how does it taste? How is it digested once it’s been attenuated? What happens to the chemicals and toxins? What happens to our bodies? Don’t be fooled: The FDA is protecting these high lobbying mega corporations who, in addition to damaging our bodies with these so-called foods, are milking the foreign countries that allow them to use their land for food production.

Even more alarming is that most citizens in this country are woefully uninformed about the predominance or dangers of genetically modified foods. Right now 60% to 70% of the ingredients found in American foods are genetically modified! [11] The United States and Canada does not require GMO foods to be labeled. In Europe, where there is far more awareness of the hazards of GMO foods, they are strictly regulated, and in many European countries, they have banned them altogether.

According to the Institute of Responsible Technology, here is a summary of what crops, foods, and food ingredients have been genetically modified as of July 2007:

Currently Commercialized GM Crops in the United States

(Number in parentheses represents the estimated percent that is genetically modified.)

- Soy (91%)
- Cotton (88%)
- Canola (80-85%)
- Corn (85%)
- Hawaiian papaya (more than 50%)
- Alfalfa, zucchini, and yellow squash (small amount)
- Tobacco (Quest brand)

Other Sources of GMOs:

- Dairy products from cows injected with rbGH
- Food additives, enzymes, flavorings, and processing agents, including the sweetener aspartame (NutraSweet) and rennet used to make hard cheeses
- Meat, eggs, and dairy products from animals that have eaten GM feed
- Honey and bee pollen that may have GM sources of pollen
- Contamination or pollination caused by GM seeds or pollen

Although these foods may not directly cause picky eating, they can certainly do our children nutritional injustice. I talk about the importance of the "one bite" concept as a strategy to overcome picky eating, and for small tummies and picky eaters, that one bite needs to pack a wallop of nutrition, far more than can come from a GMO food. GMO foods can be difficult to digest, so eliminating these foods from the diet will promote stronger metabolic absorption and better bowel functioning.

For more information on this important issue, go to

www.seedsofdeception.com

www.thefutureoffood.com

Dairy

The benefits of dairy have been exaggerated by an industry that continues to lobby the government with the belief that dairy is a necessary staple in our diet. The state of Wisconsin alone makes around $40,000 per minute from dairy revenue. [12] People believe the "Got Milk" commercials are public service messages, and that their bones will crumble and degenerate if they do not consume three servings of dairy every day. The truth is that cow's milk is a very non-absorbable version of calcium; meant to be digested by a calf with four stomachs. As Homo sapiens, we have little genetic similarities to bovines. In its raw version, the natural digestive enzymes in milk help to break down proteins and sugars, but with the destructions of enzymes through pasteurization, the body cannot properly metabolize all of the potential benefits of milk. This commonly leads to digestive disorders and mucous build up, causing countless ear, sinus, and respiratory tract infections that plague children throughout their childhood.

However, there are few foods more perfect than organic butter. All hail Julia Child for opening our eyes and stomachs to this delicious and nutritious food! Healthy fats, like butter, provide the building blocks for cell membranes as well as work as a vehicle for hormones to travel throughout your body. They act as carriers for vitamins A, D, E, and K. Real butter fans know that there is nothing quite as disgusting as margarine or worse yet, fake butter! And that oily colored substance that makes your whole house smell when someone pops popcorn in the microwave… yuck. Butter makes everything taste good AND it's so good for you, especially for children with developing brains.

There are so many negative food trends that have taken hold in our society, but few have done more harm than the hysteria surrounding fat. Altered and low fat foods are not only overly processed, they taste terrible, and they leave our brains and bodies starved for the healthy fats they need to function and grow properly. There's a reason why you are still hungry after eating "low-fat" foods. Your body knows it needs healthy fats! Some children who have trouble with supermarket and even health food store milk products, thrive on raw milk. For information on safety and availability, visit www.realmilk.com.

Soy

In 2005, Dr. Kaayla Daniel, PhD, CCN, published *The Whole Soy Story* (New Trends Publishing, Inc.) In this well researched and brilliantly organized book, Dr. Daniel presented some fascinating points about this food that we've been brainwashed into believing was our dietary savior. The following points are all taken from her book:

- The soy industry has falsified and manipulated studies reporting on soy's health benefits.
- Soy is a leading contributor of estrogen dominance. Its goitrogens, which are naturally occurring substances, interfere with the function of the thyroid gland, and its isoflavones affect hormones and reproduction.
- Soy is one of the top eight allergens.
- The oxalates and phytates in soy block absorption of calcium, zinc, and iron in the body.
- Soy is a known protease and trypsin inhibitor, which means that it can contribute to digestive abnormalities, poor protein digestion, and stress on the pancreas.

Many well meaning vegetarian parents do their children a disservice by feeding them large amounts of soy isolate protein. Malabsorption is a great concern for these growing bodies, and without the proper enzymes present in the digestive system, soy can leave many children deprived of nutrients. Unfortunately, soy is in many foods, and is difficult to avoid. The concern for the picky eater is that if digestive enzymes are obstructed, the foods eaten with the soy will not provide a metabolic benefit. Unless there is a true allergy or sensitivity, soy does not need to be completely eliminated, but it is best to be a limited part of your child's overall diet. If your child is allergic or sensitive to milk products, instead of using soy replacements, consider using nut, rice, or coconut milk alternatives. For more information on soy and diet, Dr. Daniels recommends the FAQ section on the website www.soyfreesolutions.com.

Gluten
(Wheat, Rye, Barley, Spelt, Kamut, and some Oats)

Gluten, the protein found in many grains, is also found in huge numbers of processed foods in this country. If the gluten is not fully digested, the undigested particles can trigger an immune response in the body. Celiac disease, a sometimes inherited autoimmune disease, in which the lining (villi) of the small intestines become damaged from eating gluten, is now believed to be affecting one in every 133 adults in North America. [13] People with Celiac disease are unable to absorb vital nutrients: protein, vitamins, and minerals. The symptoms of Celiac disease include cramping, abdominal pain, diarrhea, skin rashes, anemia, failure to thrive, weight loss, and possible constipation. Some doctors are slow to diagnose the problem, and tend to wait until the disease is advanced before it is diagnosed and properly treated.

When people, especially kids, don't like certain foods, we chalk it up to being picky. But it could be an unconscious rejection of a food to which the body is sensitive or intolerant. Conversely, some kids crave and are addicted to the foods that are actually making them sick. Many people with Celiac disease have an addiction to gluten. The bottom line is that if you suspect that your child may have a gluten intolerance or allergy, he or she should be tested immediately by a qualified medical practitioner with a strong understanding of gluten intolerance.

Corn and High Fructose Corn Syrup (HFCS)

Corn

There are several reasons for limiting, not just HFCS, but corn from the diet. Modern varieties of corn are genetically modified, high in sugar, poor sources of protein, and may be mold infested, promoting the increase of intestinal bugs in the GI tract. Corn contains a large amount of phytate, a strong chelator, which inhibits the absorption of important minerals like calcium, magnesium, iron, and zinc. The original corn plant, maize, started off as one of nature's premier food sources. Once a wonderful starch packed with nutrition, the only nutrient dense versions of corn left are found in rare heirloom plants. As the demand for cheap sources of sugar grew, corn seeds were hijacked by genetic engineering and the high fructose corn syrup food industry, which is now a $2.6 billion dollar business. [14] Corn's original identity as a source of protein and nutrients was gone.

High Fructose Corn Syrup

When most people think of sugar, they don't think of corn, because historically, sugar came from sugar cane or beets. Today, however, due to the lower production costs, more processed foods are sweetened with sugar made from corn, otherwise known as high fructose corn syrup or HFCS. Since production began in the 1970's, the use of HFCS has grown at enormous rates, from less than three million short tons in 1980 to almost 8 million short tons in 1995. The bottom line is that Americans now consume more HFCS than sugar. [15]

Since HFCS is a liquid, it is easy to blend into soft drinks, energy drinks, sweetened yogurt, and processed foods like ketchup, crackers, bread, soups, cereals, and canned goods.

According to the U.S. Department of Agriculture, in 2001 Americans consumed almost 63 pounds of HFCS. HFCS causes numerous problems in the body. It does not stimulate the pancreas to produce insulin, making it harder to regulate blood sugar levels, and fails to increase the production of leptin, an important hormone that regulates appetite and metabolism. The fructose in HFCS also drains the body of magnesium, thus depleting calcium absorption. Large amounts of fructose can overload the intestine's ability to absorb carbohydrates, causing cramps, bloating, and loose stools, a problem since so many baked goods are loaded with HFCS. Unlike glucose, which can be metabolized by any cell in the body, fructose can only be metabolized in the liver. Excessive amounts of HFCS cause the liver to dump more fat into the bloodstream, and may be contributing to the soaring obesity rates in the United States.

High fructose corn syrup is to corn what rubbing alcohol is to Vodka. Vodka is distilled in a way that the body knows how to utilize it, but if you were to drink rubbing alcohol you would get very ill. The empty nutrition of most corn, combined with the toxic introduction of chemicals, is compounded in our children's diet, as it is added in the least suspecting of places. The body does not register high fructose corn syrup as food, so it takes in the calories, but doesn't fill any nutritional needs. Because it's not digested, it is also very addictive. This is a major attraction to the junk food addicted child. I have many parents who tell me that once they eliminated HFCS, their children become more interested in other foods.

Case Study: Addicted to HFCS

Benjamin, age nine, came to our practice as a child with extreme ADHD, asthma, and headaches. He had huge dark circles under his eyes and was painfully skinny. His pediatrician told the parents to give him tons of high calorie junk food to help put on some pounds. Ben was on large dosages of Adderall. His parents were scared—they could look into his eyes and see that that their son was not healthy.

I first met Ben's parents in my office. They had already met with my husband, who examined Ben, and decided to run a series of tests that would determine his individual treatment plan. In the meantime, we needed to take a hard look at Ben's diet. I could tell they were already apprehensive of what I was going to tell them to do. Ben's parents had very little money, and were already under a lot of stress.

Ben cried a lot as a baby, was on formula at a young age, and quickly graduated to Pediasure (both foods have large amounts of high fructose corn syrup [HFCS]). My husband's directions were simple, "Get him off of corn." There were many more foods we would have liked to eliminate from Ben's diet, but his parents were very young, completely uneducated about food, and at that time, could not afford to switch to a completely organic diet.

I told the parents that while we were waiting for the test results, we were going to take one food out of Ben's diet. They were so happy. How hard could ONE food be? The food I asked them to remove was high-fructose corn syrup, and I spent the next hour letting them know which foods they would find it in, and how to replace it with a healthier alternative. The parents, anxious to have a healthy son, dove right in.

Benjamin was a big soda drinker, so his parents bought juice concentrates and added spoonfuls to club soda. For school, they sent iced tea that was sweetened with honey, and allowed him to have 100% fruit juice boxes. They made cookies that were still sweetened with sugar, but with no corn syrup. Because money was a big issue for the family, they couldn't afford many things at the health food store that were naturally without HFCS, but they did splurge on a few items, and ketchup was one of them. Every label was read and they stayed very true to our request.

One month later, I heard from Benjamin's mom. She said she had a completely different child. His breathing had never been better, there were no headaches, and his teacher was sending home positive notes. The best part was that being nine, Ben was old enough to know the difference in the way he felt. Taking out the HFCS in his diet didn't feel like a sacrifice. He was still getting his favorite foods, but presented in a healthier way. After the test results came back, we were able to refine Ben's diet a little more, and help his body catch up on the nutrition it lost from years of empty calories. Within a year, Ben was medication-free, and had gained solid, healthy weight from his new diet.

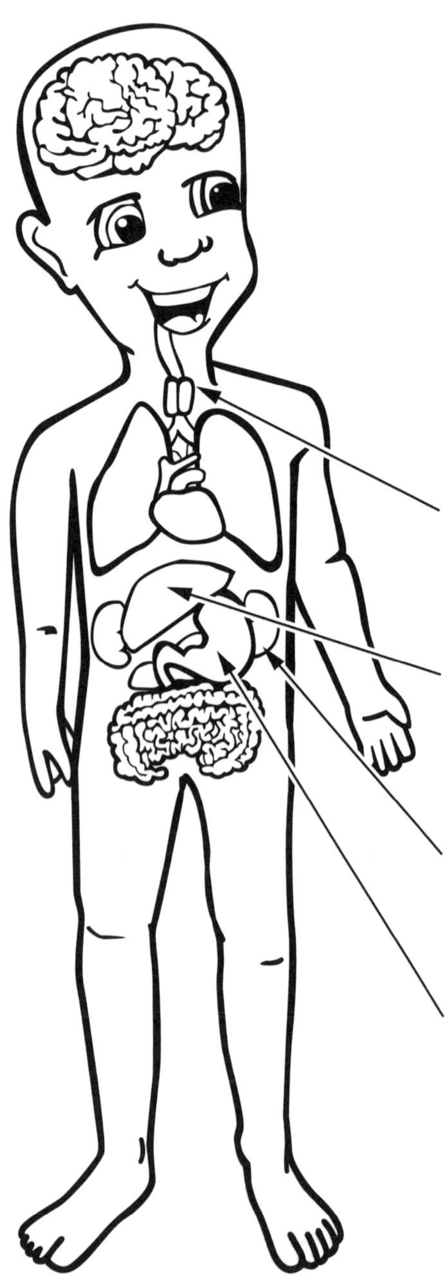

General Health
Decreased energy levels

Brain
Poor focus, concentration, and memory
Altered mood, sleep issues

Ears and Nasal
Respiratory issues, chronic colds, ear and sinus infections

Throat
Sore throats, acid reflux

Thymus
Weakened immune system, decreased resistance to viruses and bacteria, increased allergies

Liver
Decreased ability to eliminate toxins, increased risk of obesity, problems with energy metabolism, digestion, processing and distribution of nutrients

Pancreas
Digestion issues, blood sugar fluctuations and increased risk of diabetes, low cellular energy

Stomach
Poor digestion, acid reflux, and abdominal pain

Intestines
Malabsorption of nutrients, leaky gut, irritable bowel syndrome, constipation, diarrhea, increased risk of Candida

Exploring the Body: Transforming Food into Energy and The Effect of Food on the Body's Systems

The human body is a constant marvel and a truly amazing machine. The scope of its brilliant design is beyond our imagination to conceive. The body's innate wisdom and mechanisms effortlessly and continually metabolize energy, purge waste, and repair cellular tissue. It asks very little in return for carrying us throughout each day: Water, sunlight, exercise, and enough nutrition to support its functions.

The nutrition that comes from food is the basis for all functions in the body. Without proper nutrition, cells will not have energy, enzymes cannot be formed, hormones cannot work, and no tissue can be built. So how does it all work? And what does any of it have to do with picky eating?

The Digestive System

The purpose of the digestive system is to break down the foods we eat—fats, carbohydrates, and proteins—into usable components for the body. During the digestive process, carbohydrates and fats are transformed into simple glucose molecules that are delivered to the blood through the villi in the small intestine. From there, the blood delivers the glucose molecules to the cells through the walls of capillary blood vessels. Once inside the cell, the glucose is absorbed by the cell mitochondria, the energy powerhouse of the cell. In the mitochondria, glucose is converted to ATP, a form of chemical energy, through a series of enzyme-catalyzed chemical reactions in a process known as the Krebs cycle. The ATP energy is the fuel for every cellular process of the human body. The saying, "You are what you eat," is powerfully true.

Digestive action begins in the mouth. Chewing (mastication) and the chemical action of the salivary enzymes start to break down the food. After being chewed and swallowed, the food enters the esophagus, a long tube that runs from the mouth to the stomach. The esophagus uses rhythmic, muscular "waves" to force food from the throat into the stomach, like squeezing a tube of toothpaste. This muscle movement gives us the ability to eat or drink even when we're upside down. (This explains why kids can drink juice boxes standing on their heads!)

Everything you eat ends up in the stomach. Think of the stomach like a washing machine, but instead of hot water, it uses gastric acid, churning and mixing the food with acids and enzymes.

The glands in the adult stomach produce about three quarts of gastric acid every day! Unlike your washing machine, however, the goal is to break down the food into smaller and smaller pieces. Water and alcohol can be absorbed directly from the stomach—everything else has to be totally broken down and converted to its basic unit. About four hours after your child says, "I'm finished. May I be excused, please?" the food, now the consistency of thick slurry, slowly slides into the small intestine through the esophageal ring, a muscular ring that separates the stomach and the first part of the small intestine.

Inside the small intestine, enzymes and chemicals break down and mix up what now resembles a semi-liquid soup known as "Chyme." Most of the digestion and absorption of food occurs in the small intestine, a 20' twisting tube that looks a lot like one of the waterslides at an amusement park. The walls of the small intestine are lined with millions of tiny "fingers" called villi, and they, in turn, are covered with even tinier projections called microvillus. The villi are hungry sponges—absorbing nutrients and passing them into the superhighway of the bloodstream.

After traveling through the small intestine, what's left of the food passes into the large intestine. These are the true "leftovers." Microbes in the large intestine help to break down the undigested materials. The main job of the large intestine is to remove water and salts (electrolytes), and to form solid waste that can be excreted. The remaining contents of the large intestine are moved toward the rectum, where feces are stored until they leave the body as a bowel movement. The bowel movement holds many clues to the overall health of the digestive system, and to the health of the body in general. Although most mainstream medical practitioners pay little attention, we use stool testing as an important diagnostic tool in our patient intake process, including severe picky eaters.

If your picky eater shows signs of poor digestion, you may want to contact a natural medicine specialist for a stool evaluation. A great place to start is www.genovadiagnostics.com. They do an excellent digestive stool analysis that includes anaerobic bacteria, yeast, and other absorption and metabolic markers. There are multiple reasons why the digestive system functions poorly, and it's important to know how it may be affecting your child's diet and attitude towards food. Evaluating your child's bowel activity lends many clues to the health of his/her digestive system.

Signs of Good Digestion	Signs of Poor Digestion
1 to 2 bowel movements a day Medium brown in color Well formed Sinks to the bottom of the toilet Smooth	Blood or mucus Green in color Extremely light (tan) or extremely dark brown Chunks of food Floating Oily Not eliminating daily/or Diarrhea

Leaky Gut

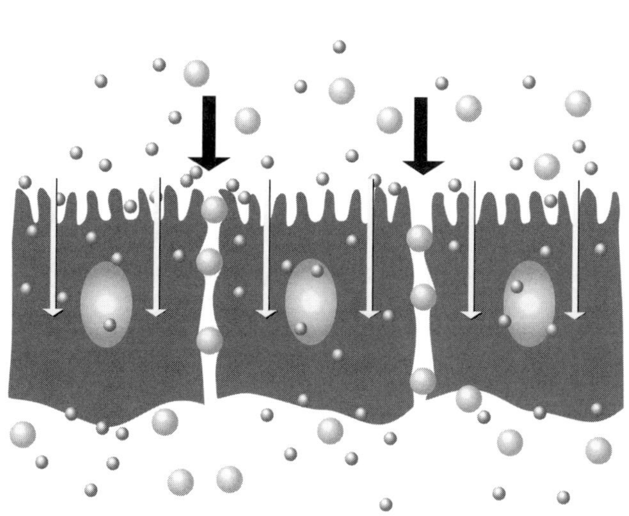

Normal Gut

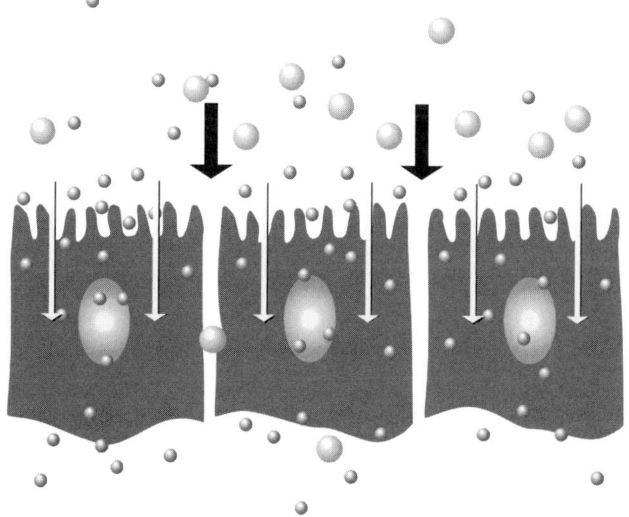

Digestive Problems: Leaky Gut

Digestive problems can be caused by an overabundance of "abnormal bacteria" or other microbes. Abnormal bacteria can be aerobic (they need oxygen to survive) or anaerobic (they can live without oxygen). Some of these bacteria produce toxins that punch holes in the intestinal tract and can contribute to a condition known as "leaky gut" and malabsorption of food. Leaky gut occurs when undigested food particles leak through these holes in the intestinal wall into the bloodstream. The immune system doesn't recognize these large particles as food and attacks the food particles in the same way it would bacterial invaders by forming IgG or IgA antibodies. Because the IgG is a delayed immune system reaction, there is not always a clear link between the offending food, the symptoms that occur, and the food hypersensitivities that develop. Lab testing can be a good start in pinpointing the foods that may be causing immune and intestinal upset, but an inexpensive and often more reliable option is to use a food diary to keep track of foods that cause digestive or other problems.

The use of natural anti-bacterials can be used to clear specific or general bacteria in the body. Elimination of certain foods may become necessary in the short term while restoring the natural balance of bacteria in the intestines. If you suspect that your child does have food intolerances, a great resource for understanding how elimination diets can help restore digestive system health is the groundbreaking book, *Is This Your Child?* by Doris J. Rapp, MD. (www.drrapp.com)

Probiotics

Probiotics are one of the mainstays to healing the gut and reducing acid reflux. Probiotics are microorganisms that are naturally found in the human gut. They are also called "friendly bacteria" or "good bacteria." Probiotics act as a protective barrier in the intestinal tract that protect the villi and intestinal wall from bacterial invaders.

Many grocery store yogurt brands have jumped on the probiotic movement and added probiotics to their products. There are many strains of probiotics, however, and the cheaper and more popular strains tend to use poor quality ingredients. Some of the organic versions are good, but taking a probiotic pill is still something to discuss with your natural health care practitioner. A great natural and inexpensive way to get probiotics is through cultured vegetables. Cultured vegetables are similar to sauerkrauts, made the "old fashioned" way from salt or with probiotic culture starters that you can get from www.bodyecology.com. Cultured vegetables not only give you probiotics, but also digestive enzymes, B vitamins, and many other nutrients. For more information on probiotics, go to www.westonaprice.org.

A Case History: The Hockey Mom

Nine-year old Sarah lived with her family in an extremely wealthy suburb of Chicago, and I was aware that the community tended to be affluent and very competitive. During his first marriage, my husband raised his own sons in the same area, and he confirmed that there was a great deal of pressure to have your children active in sports, music, dance, or other types of extracurricular activity. Because of her health issues, Sarah was tested for IgG food sensitivities. The test results showed that Sarah was exceptionally reactive to about ten different foods. After sharing the test results with the mom over the phone, I began counseling her on how to remove these foods from Sarah's diet.

After about 20 minutes of instruction, she finally interrupted with, "I just have to tell you right now, that I'm not going to do this."

"Really?" I was shocked. The test we performed on Sarah was not inexpensive, and I was perplexed why anyone would do a test, get the results back, and not try to amend the situation, especially when it was clear that Sarah was not well.

"Listen," she said angrily, "I have two boys in hockey. They have practice every night, and if I can't pick up the food on the way to a practice or a game, it's not going to happen."

"But you can eat out, you just need to have more foods prepared to take with you for Sarah," I pleaded.

"No, maybe later. I just have way too much going on in my life," and she quickly ended the conversation.

I hung up in shock and started to cry. Her daughter was sick, and would get sicker if she didn't remove the offending foods from Sarah's diet. I couldn't believe that her sons' hockey games were prioritized above her daughter's health. Games and events will come and go, and although I understand the value of convenience, I also understand the importance of health. I have seen many adult versions of the "Sarahs of the world" suffering from chronic illness. As children, they did not have high-risk or serious illnesses that would force their parents to pay attention—and because their medical needs were diet and nutrition-based, they were easy to ignore. Over time, as they got older and sicker, they became extremely susceptible to autoimmune diseases. In our practice, my husband and I see these children as adults, battling everything from Celiac disease to MS. All in all: a high price to pay for a hockey game.

Digestive Problems: Grazing

Grazing is the habit of eating very small amounts of food consistently throughout the day. Grazing was a fad, thought to be "healthier" than eating defined meals at regular intervals. Children that are allowed to graze rarely get a full meal, and never get the opportunity to be hungry. Grazing makes it harder to get picky eaters to try new foods, but there are biomedical problems with grazing as well. If there is a predisposition to leaky gut, the constant flushing of food into the intestines can lead to breaks in the intestinal wall. The food particles that leak out are treated as a foreign substance by the body, because they are no longer "where they belong" in the body. In response to the continual influx of foreign food particles, the immune system becomes stressed, and goes into hyper-drive—constantly pumping out antibodies. The food antibodies can lead to IgG food hypersensitivity, often known as food intolerances, and can be a precursor to autoimmune disease.

Another biomedical issue that can be precipitated by grazing is a decline in digestion. Grazing leads to the continual stimulation of the pancreas to produce digestive enzymes. If the pancreas is already stressed, or genetically prone to weakness, grazing further complicates the ability of the pancreas to do its job.

The Rotation Diet

A rotation diet is one method of treating IgG intolerances. Eating the same foods day after day means that those same foods are repeatedly moving through the intestinal tract, and if leaky gut is already a problem, the immune system will constantly pump out antibodies against the offending foods that it sees as "the enemy." Eating the problem foods no more than once every four days can give the immune and the digestive system time to heal and restore equilibrium. The three days off gives the body a chance to rebuild antibodies, and allows the kidneys to clear the antibodies from the blood.

Digestive Enzymes

Amylase, the body enzyme that breaks down starch into sugar, can be depleted in newborns of mothers who ate a lot of carbohydrates during pregnancy. These children are born with a potential deficiency in carbohydrate digestion. An overabundance of carbohydrates in a baby or toddler's diet will then begin to stress the ability of the pancreas to produce insulin. Without insulin, the body can't metabolize sugar (glucose) into energy and clear glucose from the bloodstream. Part of the reason for the skyrocketing rates of diabetes in kids is the carbohydrate-rich diet they are eating, and their long-term inability to regulate glucose by insulin.

The lack of enzymes for digestion can potentially lead to malnutrition, as the body is not able to break down, digest, or absorb the nutrients from the food. The rotting of the undigested food in the stomach leads to acid reflux—just the opposite of what we are led to believe! Antacids only intensify and mask the true problem. For years, my son Joey was in pain when he tried to lie down and go to bed each night. The only way he could fall asleep was to totally sit up. Not knowing any better, I would give him acid reflux medication. The medication only added to the real problem. Joey lacked digestive enzymes. (This is very common in people with Type A blood, which Joey has.) Without enough digestive enzymes, he couldn't properly break down his food. The undigested food would "rot" and release an acid in his throat. In our clinic, we see hundreds of patients every year that are able to get off of reflux medications in exchange for digestive enzymes at each meal. You can learn more about the role of enzymes at www.enzymedica.com.

The Detoxification System

Detoxification is a complicated two-part process that our body uses to eliminate waste, toxins, and to convert fat-soluble materials into water-soluble materials for excretion. The simple way to put it is that detoxification is the process that gets rid of not just the poop, but all the "junk" and toxins that the body is exposed to each day. Unless you are living in a bubble, it is impossible to avoid them, and even if you are living in a bubble, the plastics in your bubble are probably out gassing PCB's! Our air, water, and especially our foods are not the same as they were 100 years ago. Today, we are routinely exposed to thousands of chemicals every day. For instance, aluminum is now found in vaccines as a replacement to the preservative thimerasol. Aluminum inhibits cellular and metabolic processes in the nervous system and other tissues, and increases the permeability of the blood-brain barrier. Aluminum shows up in many foods including soy, table salt, and tap water. It is also present in all chicken feed that is not organic, which means that most processed chicken also contains aluminum.

Aluminum enters your food or beverage through canned products with the addition of tin. Even more dangerous is the use of aluminum cookware and foil. Found in nearly every kitchen, Americans add aluminum to hot dishes and baked goods daily. When you realize how many toxins and dangerous chemicals we, and our children, are routinely exposed to every day, you can appreciate just how critical the detoxification system is to long-term health and wellness.

Our body's ability to detoxify is largely influenced by our genetics. The liver is the super-star of the de-tox system. The liver filters up to two quarts of blood a minute for detoxification. It manufactures about one quart of bile each day, which "carries" many fat-soluble toxins and cholesterol into the intestine for processing, where they are absorbed by fiber and eliminated. And finally, the liver is responsible for a two-phase conversion process that neutralizes unwanted chemical compounds—everything from natural body chemicals to pesticides, drugs, alcohol, caffeine, preservatives, artificial flavors and colors, heavy metals—all of the hidden side effects of daily life.

A healthy immune system is properly balanced between these two phases. Phase I can directly neutralize many substances, but some chemicals and toxins must be converted to an intermediate form known as free radicals that can be far more lethal than the original version of the substance. If the intermediate free radicals left from Phase I are not quickly and fully eliminated during Phase II, they can cause significant damage to the body.

Issues with detoxification are often completely overlooked by traditional medicine and even some holistic practitioners. "Natural" medical doctors often use harsh measures to rid the body of toxins, and in many cases, without determining if the two phases are working in proper balance. If Phase I is working overtime, and Phase II can't keep up, there is a build-up of toxins and free radicals in the body.

Our hormones and neurotransmitters: dopamine, epinephrine, and nor epinephrine are also regulated by the detoxification system. Many people and children with hormone imbalances have difficulty with their detoxification system, as hormone imbalances are not simply limited to glandular irregularity. It's not just about production; it's also about elimination.

Failure to keep the de-toxification system running smoothly can weaken the immune system. Most epidemiologists and cancer researchers agree that between 80-90% of cancers are linked to environmental effects—including lifestyle factors such as diet, alcohol, and tobacco as well as radiation, infectious agents, and substances in the air, water, and soil. [16] Poorly functioning detoxification and immune systems add significantly to the cancer risk.

The first step for anyone wishing to rid their bodies of toxicity is to get the liver and kidneys functioning properly. Many health professionals and patients work backwards—foods such as cilantro will bind with heavy metals, but if the detoxification system has any blockages, the metals will reabsorb and cause further complications. Artichokes, especially the Jerusalem artichoke, are an excellent way to support the liver. Beets will also clean out the liver, and parsley will clean the kidneys.

Constipation is your biggest blockage to proper detoxification. High fibrous foods such as berries and most vegetables will assist in purging foods out of the intestines, but the most important tool, by far, is clean filtered water. Not sure how much to drink? Take your body-weight, cut it in half, and that is the minimum number of ounces of water you should drink in a day. For picky eaters, water is so important. Soda will dehydrate and de-mineralize the body, and for adults, coffee and tea act as a diuretic, which may cause you to purge liquid before it has an opportunity to hydrate the body's tissues. A well-hydrated diet rich in natural fiber and organic vegetables is critical to long-term health and wellness and the best foundation you can give to your child.

The Immune System

When did the American population stop taking ownership of their health, and stop asking, "Why do we get sick?" When did we just accept that diseases like cancer were an inevitable part of life, and if we rolled the dice and got ill, we were just "unlucky?" Even if you're "lucky" enough not to have cancer, are you, or your children, one of the millions of Americans with a recurrent infection, food allergies, fatigue, or low energy? Do you ever stop to wonder WHY?

The answer is directly related to the immune system, but this profound connection is truly not understood by traditional medicine. At our clinic, Dr. Hicks routinely runs standard immune panels on patients. The labs call us, perplexed at the order—as if he is the only doctor around who makes these requests. This should be the FIRST place any doctor looks. To fully comprehend the immune system would take more than a small chapter in this book, but understanding its relationship to food and picky eating is pertinent.

Our immune system is a comprehensive security system, employing complex defensive and offensive resources in various parts of the body. Our focus here is on the T-helper cells—and the immune messengers known more broadly as the cytokines. The cytokines are responsible for most of the immunity-related and allergic type responses of the immune system. The T-helper 1 cytokines produce a pro-inflammatory response to pathogens (invaders). To put it simply, the immune system should operate like a teeter-totter, shifting from the T-suppressor cells fighting viruses and cancers to T-helper cells battling bad bacteria and creating the appropriate antibodies to stop infections and foreign invaders. The T-Helper immune shift may be triggered by chronic leaky gut and that can throw antibody production into overdrive, creating food allergies or intolerances, and this chronic imbalance is often the catalyst for autoimmune disease.

Neurotransmitters and Methylation

What does food (and picky eating) have to do with the neurotransmitters? Neurotransmitters are substances that act to tell our senses, our brains, our muscles, and our organs what to do, and they are in constant communication with other parts of the body. The most common neurotransmitters are dopamine, epinephrine, nor epinephrine, and serotonin. They are generally associated with brain function: mood focus, concentration, anxiety, obsessions, and mood disorders like bi-polar disease.

Believe it or not, the gut contains 100 million neurons—more than the spinal cord. Major neurotransmitters like serotonin, dopamine, glutamate, norephinephrine, and nitric oxide are in the gut. There are also dozens of small proteins, called neuropeptides, along with the major cells of the immune system, in the gut as well. Enkephalins (a member of the endorphins family) are also in the gut. The gut is a rich source of benzodiazepines; the family of psychoactive chemicals that include popular drugs like Valium, Xanax, and other mood stabilizers, but every cell in the body has receptors for these neurotransmitter compounds, so their impact is felt throughout all of the body's systems.

Methylation is a very important process that modulates reactions in the body. The methylation process plays a role in epigenome function (which turns genes on and off), neurotransmitter function, cellular development, detoxification of chemicals, and homocysteine (amino acid) conversion. The enzymes that control the methylation process are determined by your DNA, and affected by your environment. Methylation functions poorly in children with autism spectrum disorder, and people with DNA deficiencies. Impaired methylation can be detrimental to many functions in the human body, and potentially be the genesis of disease.

Vitamins and amino acids that aid in methylation are B-12 (must be methylcobalamin), folinic acid, and DMG (dimethylglycine). These vitamins and amino acids are frequently deficient in picky eaters because of the lack of quality protein and green vegetables in their diet. Here are the top foods rich in the vitamins and amino acids that aid in the process of methylation. (Source provided by George Mateljan at www.whfoods.com.)

- Calf's liver
- Snapper fish
- Venison
- Salmon
- Beef
- Lamb
- Romaine lettuce
- Spinach (and most dark greens)
- Asparagus
- Broccoli
- Cauliflower
- Beets
- Lentils
- Black, Pinto, Garbanzo, Navy, and Kidney Beans

Why Does My Child Act Like an Addict When He Can't Get His Favorite Foods?

Excitotoxins

Savvy marketers have dubbed it, "The Big Mac Attack" and promise, "Betcha' can't eat just one!"

The marketing is actually correct in that cravings for certain foods can seem like an "attack." The responsible culprits have been labeled as excitotoxins and are clearly explained in Dr. Ruseell Blaylock's book, *Excitotoxins: The Taste that Kills*. Some of the most widely used excitotoxins are: Monosodium Glutamate (MSG), high fructose corn syrup (HFCS), artificial food coloring, nitrates/nitrites, and artificial sweeteners. Excitotoxins are chemicals or amino acids that disrupt neurotransmitters, and can literally "excite" them to death. These substances actually trick the brain to make the food seem, "flavor enhanced." In small amounts, the body can detoxify these chemicals, but the American diet has exploded in its use of excitotoxins such as MSG, Aspartame, and other "natural flavorings," compounding the toxicity and symptoms of these silent chemical bombs.

These chemicals put our taste buds into hyper-drive and ignite cravings. The interesting discovery is that when manufacturers use two different excitotoxins in one food, the effects are not just doubled, but increase exponentially. For instance, the incredibly popular "energy drinks" combine caffeine, food coloring, high fructose corn syrup, and artificial sweeteners! Talk about a toxic jolt to the system. It is impossible to fully enjoy the taste of real food when one's body has adjusted to hyper-flavor. Every week in my clinic, I speak to someone with excitotoxin addictions. The mom who "has to have" her diet coke, the child who will only eat a certain brand of chicken nuggets, the teenager who eats an entire bag of flavored potato chips without coming up for air.

Food coloring, in most artificial forms, is a petrochemical. These chemicals damage liver and kidney function. How many of us would order our child's birthday cake with red or blue frosting if we knew what was really in those food dyes? The increasing popularity of brightly colored drinks, candy like Skittles, and the strange "blue ketchup" is a startling example that in our society, we think that children's food choices have to be entertaining before kids will eat them. Mealtime is driven by the need to "wow" kids and create an "event," rather than just a healthy meal. Children aren't given a chance to try new foods, as parents all too often give in to childish demands in order to keep peace at the table.

The Candida Factor & Bacteria Overgrowth

The majority of Americans have rampant yeast and bacteria overgrowth. The three big reasons for this are a lack of quality probiotics in the American diet, an overabundance of antibiotics for children, even in infancy, and a diet rich in yeast and bacteria feeding foods.

Throughout Europe, Australia, and New Zealand, ingesting probiotics is not only prescribed by medical doctors, but also rich in common foods. Freeze dried powdered probiotics are available in some yogurt brands here in the United States, but the probiotics are usually dead before they ever make it to your refrigerator, or simply small, or unvaried in supply. There are many different strains of probiotics and a comprehensive digestive stool analysis can label the strains and their levels in the body. Probiotics form a protective lining in our small intestine, and prevent food allergies and intolerances. They also aid in absorption and control yeast and bacteria levels.

Yeast levels rise when children are given antibiotics without the addition of a probiotic to control yeast growth. We have good and bad bacteria in our gut at all times, but when bad bacteria gets out of control in our body and we fight it (sometimes rightfully so) with an antibiotic, we equally destroy the good bacteria. Antibiotics should never be prescribed without the follow up of a good probiotic. This concern is heightened in babies who need special strains of bifidus bacteria. Failure to proactively treat with the probiotics creates a poor foundation for their digestive system.

Our food choices have been decreasing in probiotics and increasing in yeast and bacteria forming foods. There is a growing awareness of the benefit of naturally fermented foods, but a large percentage of the population is unaware of this important diet component. The use of naturally fermented foods is an alternative to taking a powdered probiotic.

My personal story with this is powerful, because although I put years and tremendous effort into healing my son's food intolerances, the addition of fermented vegetables was the missing piece of this food puzzle. When I added homemade sauerkraut (made with salt or probiotics, NOT vinegar) as a daily "supplement" to Joey's diet, he went from 50 to 0 food intolerances in a matter of six months. Because this is a book specifically on strategies for overcoming picky eating, I am not going to take too much time teaching you about the benefits of one of the most difficult foods to introduce to a picky eater. However, I urge you to visit www.westonaprice.org to learn more.

Aside from using probiotics as a barrier to prevent yeast and bacterial overgrowth, it is equally important not to further feed what is active already. Yeast and bacteria will die without their favorite foods, and that is why so many kids crave the sugar, fructose, vinegar (usually a kid favorite in forms of pickles and ketchup), and corn products (especially those that are GMO) that keep the yeast and bacteria alive and growing. Many wonderful natural enzymes can be used to destroy yeast, but I strongly urge against using anti-fungals that will push yeast into the liver and cause stress on the body.

Peptide Addictions

Due to the lack of, or a shortage of, the digestive enzyme Dipeptidyl Peptidase IV, two food proteins, gluten and casein, can trick the body into processing them as an opioid drug. Opioid foods effect digestion and both neurological and sensory processing. Because they are addictive, these foods often make up the majority of a picky eater's diet. Gluten is the protein found in wheat, oats, rye, spelt, Kamut, and a few other uncommon grains. Casein is the protein in animal milk. A child who is strongly affected by these opioids will automatically self-limit his/her diet to an extremely small amount of food options. This is a serious factor to deal with, because it will become even more difficult to introduce new foods if your eater is addicted to these opioid proteins. Here are some physical signs that may help you determine if your picky eater is addicted to gluten and casein, keeping in mind that he/she may only be affected by a few of these symptoms:

- Hyperactivity
- Moodiness
- "Spaced out" behavior
- Poor memory
- Sleep problems
- Poor organizational skills
- Inability to multi-task
- Never feeling full after eating
- Poor urine/stool control
- Craves only gluten and casein
- Extreme picky eating

Switching to the Gluten-Free Casein-Free (GFCF)diet is one of the first things to consider when tackling a picky eating situation where you suspect that peptide addictions are a problem. A good source of information is the website www.GFCFDiet.com. The following story is an all-too common case study of a child that was addicted to opiate foods.

Case Study: Peter and His Pepsi

Peter was an eight year-old boy with non-verbal autism. When I met Peter, he was very sick with digestive problems. He had rampant yeast and bacteria growing in his gut, and was constantly plagued by gastric reflux. Peter was blessed with parents who loved him dearly. His dad traveled a lot, however, and his mom was doing her best to raise Peter and his younger brother. During the initial consultation, I noted that his mom had a definite, "been there, tried that" attitude. While still hopeful that there might be a magic bullet out there, nothing I said convinced her that Peter's health could improve.

One of the first things I recommended to his parents was a strict gluten and casein free (GFCF) diet. Many children with Peter's symptoms improve dramatically when they go on this diet. Peter started on the GFCF diet, and when I called to check on his status, I was greatly surprised when his mother said that he had just "stopped eating." Peter was not an exceptionally thin child, and it didn't make sense to me that he was eating "nothing" at all.

Concerned, my first question was regarding liquid intake. There is a very different and fearful timeline when a child is not drinking anything. Our bodies can survive without food for much longer than we realize, but not without liquids. To my relief, his mom confirmed that Peter was drinking fluids.

"Water?" I asked.

"Well, no, Pepsi."

"Does he drink water?" I repeated.

She countered with, "He will, but he likes Pepsi."

Puzzled, I switched to questioning his solids intake.

"What foods does he eat?"

Peter's mom repeated that he wasn't eating "anything." Now more than a little confused, I tried again.

"But he drinks Pepsi?"

"Yes—Pepsi," she confirmed.

Mom's story didn't make sense. I cut our conversation short and with her permission, I called Peter's teacher, hoping for answers. I was blessed, in this case, to be working with the school system. They were aware of Peter's food issues, and were trying to help Peter and his mother.

The teacher had a totally different story. She told me that Peter was literally addicted to sugar, and that he only wanted foods that were high in sugar. Peter's teacher guessed that his mom was terribly embarrassed about his diet. It was easier for her to say that he wasn't eating "anything," because in the reality of real versus fake food, he wasn't eating anything healthy.

I called Peter's mom back, and she started to cry. She was overwhelmed with her son's autism, her husband always being gone, and the incredible burden of raising the boys by herself. So worried about not doing enough, or being enough, she was riddled with guilt, and gave her kids everything they wanted without questioning whether it was truly in their best interests. Peter's digestive aliments were caused by the food she allowed him to have, which made her feel even more guilty, and yet she couldn't bring herself to withhold the food she knew was harming him.

My message to Peter's mother was the same one I give to all my parents and to the readers of this book who are living with parental guilt. I feel qualified to deliver this message, because few parents carried a heavier guilt burden than I did. Guilt holds us back and confuses our children. It prevents us from trusting and accepting ourselves, and locks our children into a room without walls. Without boundaries and borders, they don't know where they begin or end. They don't want to be given every request they make. It leaves no room for desire or anticipation. If you constantly get everything you think you want, nothing is special or meaningful or new.
Kids should learn an appreciation for contrast, variety, anticipation, and healthful hunger. Think how much better food tastes when you are filled with hungry appreciation for the meal ahead.

I told Peter's mom that I could help, but she was going to have to be willing to say, "no" to her child and set some boundaries. Peter's brother Matthew had epilepsy, and I used his medical needs as an analogy to explain the importance of following Peter's diet.

"Everyday you get that medicine down Matthew, don't you?" I asked. She agreed, and said she was 100% committed to doing it, because his life depended on it. When a parent is so extremely sure of their actions, the child knows and feels that certainty, and after a short time, they don't put up a fight if the parent is consistent. As long as mom had any doubt about Peter's dietary needs, every meal would be a battle. When Peter's mother became convinced that food WAS her child's medicine, she could move from shaky guilt to confident warrior.

She agreed to take most of the junk out of the house, and within two months, I got this note:

"I still can't believe it every time Peter eats carrots! I never thought this was possible. It was really hard for about two weeks as he was withdrawing from the sugar. I still allowed him to have cookies and candy, but I am amazed how quickly he cooperated once he knew I was serious. I think the trick was making sure he was hungry, and wasn't snacking or getting soda to fill up on between meals."

Peter's mother saw the connection between breaking the addiction to high-sugar snacks and junk foods and being hungry enough to try new foods. By letting go of her misplaced guilt, she gave herself permission to set healthy boundaries for her children and healthy food on the table, and everyone benefited.

Part III: Strategies and Solutions for Picky Eating: My Work as a Diet Counselor

I didn't set out to become an expert on diet and nutrition. My original plan was to host a diet support group that was just for autism. But in 1997, in the small suburb of Illinois where I lived, there were not enough families with autistic children to do a full-fledged support group specifically on nutrition. I realized I could attract a larger audience by hosting a support group that promoted healthy eating for all children. The group was a hit, and reached many struggling parents. My growing expertise in specialty diets got the attention of Dr. Mercola, a local osteopath. I went to work for him counseling families on how to successfully implement diets free of chemicals, sugars, simple carbs, gluten, and dairy. With my additional experience, I branched out on my own, and began my own private practice as a diet and nutrition counselor. My work with autistic children and their parents ultimately led me to the work that I do with my husband in our holistic clinic. I am very grateful to

Dr. Mercola for the knowledge and experience I gained in his employ. However, no one was a greater teacher to me than my friend, and co-worker, Beth Van De Boom, a nutritional consultant and medical intuitive at Elementals Living.

Beth had a history of extreme digestive issues and Celiac disease that forced her to learn everything she could about food in order to stay alive. She was, and is a master of nutrition, herbs, supplements, therapeutic essential oils, and vibrational remedies. She could tell me what foods did what to the body, and could pull out an article or research to back it up. Beth and my husband still work together at Elementals Living, and I am still learning from her.

Although my counseling style has changed over the years, the most important way to help a family is to first find out where they are on the nutrition and food "roadmap." If they never plan on buying a whole organic chicken and making stock, I won't go there. Feeling overwhelmed is the beginning of giving up, so I ease into every situation, and meet families "where they are."

After their initial session, my goal is to give the parents enough steps and strategies to get them through the next two months. At that point, I like to meet with them again to assess their progress, and help them set new goals and objectives. For many, the only beginning assignment I give them is to give up high fructose corn syrup. With the elimination of that one food, they naturally pull away from other chemicals because most companies add a consortium of artificial color, flavor, and preservatives to the low-cost, high-production high fructose corn syrup food products, so the benefits are compounded when you remove it from the diet. By keeping the goal attainable, and the benefits easily measured, parents can see progress, and are often eager to do more.

I then work with families on different ways of shopping, as many are very intimidated with health food stores, knowing what products to buy, or how to choose healthy fruits and vegetables. I remember crying the first time I was in a health food store. I knew I had to read labels and didn't understand the ingredient names or what they meant. Food labels are still misleading—when it comes to packaging, the word "Natural" is incredibly confusing and often misrepresented—so it's important to shop at a store where you feel supported. Most health food or high-end grocery stores have helpful employees that can show you around the store and help you find what you need.

Once parents have seen the benefit of changes to their child's diet, I help them tap into their own intuition and confidence so they trust their feeling of knowing what the next logical step will be. The amount of books and websites on special diets, nutrition, and supplements are overwhelming and all conflicting. I have changed my opinion about certain foods consistently over the last two decades. The bottom line is that there is no one correct way to eat! There is no diet that is perfect for everyone. In order to assimilate it all, and create a model for your child, you have to follow that sense of confidence in yourself. If you question yourself, your child will question you back.

Over the years, I have worked with children with multiple food allergies to children who were on extremely strict protein and vegetable diets. Through private counseling, lectures, conferences, and pod casts, I have reached out to over 100,000 parents who were looking for answers and help. I don't claim to have all of the solutions or the ONE method that you just unfold and then, magically, your child is a healthy eater, but I do understand how many parents think and feel. I see and know their guilt, fears, and desire for change. I understand the challenge of money, time, and energy, and what is expected of them on a daily basis. I know what it's like to see your child having a temper tantrum at the table, and think, "If only I was a better mom or dad, things would be different."

Beating yourself up only perpetuates and accentuates the issues at hand. Take a deep breath. Relax into parenting. Parents have been feeding their children for thousands and thousands of years. Don't worry about what everyone else thinks. Don't feel like you have to get "everything right, right now." Do what feels comfortable to you, and the joy of eating will come back and join you for dinner at every meal.

Overview of Steps to Success

1. Imagine and identify your goal.

Imagine the thrill of your child loving a variety of foods. Create that image in your mind, and then write it down. Everyone's desire will be different, so use this only as an example:

"It would be wonderful if Jamie was eating a variety of foods that are nutritious. I'd like to introduce two new vegetables that she enjoys by the end of this month. I would also like to try the buffet at the Indian restaurant. By the end of the month, we are also going to take as much high fructose corn syrup out of our diet as we can, and as a family, we are all going to start reading labels."

2. Visit a qualified medical practitioner who has studied nutrition outside of mainstream medicine.

I recommend sending your child's stool to a lab that can properly diagnose potential imbalances of bacteria, parasites, and yeast. I also recommend doing a food antibody assessment that measures both IgE and IgG food hypersensitivities. For children with extreme digestive problems, a Celiac profile should also be done.

3. Make and be clear about the new rules.

This is vital. Everyone in the house, including the children, need to understand the new rules on food. Example:

"Jamie has to eat three bites of both a vegetable and a meat or alternate protein at dinner. No more soda will be bought for our home. If we go out, and she wants a soda, she must drink one glass of water for each glass or can of soda she drinks. If Jamie is invited to a birthday party at a fast-food restaurant, she needs to eat one serving of vegetables before she goes, then she can eat whatever she likes there."

The key to successful rule setting is to make rules that you can keep, and start with changes you know you can do. Allow for structured flexibility. You're not saying "No" unequivocally. You're saying "Yes, but…"

4. Talk to your child about the changes you wish to make.

He should not wake up one morning shocked to find that everything in the pantry is different. If your child is young or non-verbal, create a story they will understand by making a book of pictures with new foods looking tasty, and pictures of happy children eating them!

5. Find some new recipes for inspiration.

Look for cookbooks that use "whole ingredients." Recipes made with Lite Campbell soups are not healthy options. Now is a great time to visit your local health food store or search the Internet. A health food chain like Whole Foods or even your local health food store tends to be more selective about the type of cookbooks they carry, or visit your local library. Reading recipes with new ingredients is a great way to get inspired to cook healthfully!

6. Go grocery shopping with your child, especially if he/she is old enough to read or recognize words.

Have fun finding labels with wholesome ingredients. Turn the produce section into an "adventure," pick out a new vegetable to try, and make a new recipe together.

7. Be gentle on yourself when you are cooking and trying new foods.

You Tube has wonderful instructional videos or watch The Food Network for inspiration. If you have little ones who like to be in the kitchen, let them help and definitely let them watch, as that will ease the fear of the new foods for everybody!

8. Begin with the "First This, Then That" motivation strategy for dealing with the various levels of sensory defensiveness.

Determine where your child falls on the defensive spectrum and begin there.

9. Implement the "Three-Bite" rule at meals when the child grows comfortable with trying the new foods.

10. Graduate to full servings, using their "fist portion" to determine the right portion size.

Through it all, celebrate each new improvement and constantly give positive feedback to your child without making them the victim. For example:

Don't: "I'm so sorry I'm putting you through this. It must be horrible to have to eat this food."

Do: "I love how cooperative you are about this change. I know it's not what you are used to, but you ate that carrot last night like a bunny. It was amazing to watch. I could almost see the cells of your body cheering as you chewed it up."

Here's a story from a family who really embraced their "inner vegetable!"

"Dear Betsy:

I just need to thank you for your work with Kyle and Katie. I can't believe how easy it was to make the changes after we spoke with you. Once I made up my mind to do it, it just flowed. It really helped that the kids spoke with you about our plan. You totally convinced them that their bodies celebrated each time they ate a vegetable. It's hysterical to watch Kyle talk to his body. It gave them more responsibility and made it so much easier for me. We had so much fun picking out new vegetables to try and now each week we try something new. The kids take turns picking out something at the store they haven't tried before. It's not only been fun, but I have tried a bunch of new foods because of it, and can't believe how many good things I have been missing. Thanks again for your ideas!"

Understanding Taste and Texture: The Worm Story

It is human nature to fear the unknown. Predictability relaxes all children, whether it's familiar tastes or smells, but perhaps nothing is as important as the way the food feels. I am not referring to how it feels when you touch it with your fingers, but rather, how it feels in your mouth. Many parents will say to their child, "It's just a piece of chicken, what are you so afraid of?" Let's turn the tables on the parents for a moment. Who decided chicken meat is not scary and rabbit meat is? In many countries, where fish and goat are staples, the thought of eating turkey seems "scary." It's what we have been conditioned to expect that we accept. One of the biggest hurdles in conquering picky eating is to break the fear of the unfamiliar and replace it with open curiosity.

Let's have fun with this idea. Let's pretend that YOU are scooped up from your comfortable food culture and dropped down in a rural part of China. These are the healthiest people you have ever seen. Their skin, their bodies, and their minds all radiate with wellness. Now it's dinnertime, and the smells coming from the kitchen seem strange to you. You're curious, but fear starts to build in your stomach. As you sit down to dinner, you are dazzled by an assortment of foods that you are looking forward to eating, until you notice a bowl of worms. You watch in growing horror as the people around you pick up the worms and slurp them down like spaghetti. You are told that this is what everyone eats, it's how he or she stays healthy, and there is nothing scary about it. You are also told that it is extremely rude to not try everything on the table, and there may be consequences if you don't. What do you do? Your response is likely based on several factors: How hungry are you? And how many worms do you have to eat? What's going to happen to you if you don't eat any worms at all?

Let's start with the degree of hunger. If you have been eating crackers all day, and have a belly full of sugary juice, it is highly unlikely you would have any desire to even try a worm. Many children "graze" throughout the day, a habit that has become popular in the past 20 years as more "snack" foods surface. The urge to snack comes from not meeting your nutritional needs during mealtime. For example, it's lunchtime, but you are in a hurry, so you grab some chips and a bag of cookies. The body gets calories and is satiated for about an hour, but the body wanted protein, vitamins, minerals, and healthy fats and received nothing. So, the very intelligent body does the next logical thing; it gets hungry again. This is the pattern of "grazing": constantly filling the body with empty nutrition. Children rarely make it to true hunger. This creates a false sense of what hunger really is. It's also very sad, because eating a meal when you are truly hungry is extremely satisfying.

One of my favorite places for parents to try new foods is at the park. Make it a habit to pack unusual picnic items when there is no other choice then the food you brought. Allow them to play, run around, and work up an appetite, making sure to give them plenty of water for hydration. When it's time to eat, unpack the new foods and offer them. With no other choices and a hungry tummy, their chances of trying a new and different food will be greatly enhanced.

The next question in the worm story is, "How much do you have to eat?" Remember, the people in the town simply said you have to "try" everything. Trying can consist of a single crumb. A crumb may not seem substantial enough for the bother, but this is how the process of desensitization works. For a child who is an extremely picky eater, (especially one with a learning disability), even if the crumb simply touches their mouth, it's enough for a reward.

And rewarding leads us to our next question, which is, "What is the consequence if I don't eat the worm?" While I never endorse punishment of any kind in relation to food, withholding other foods, although it may seem punishing to the child, is mandatory to the motivational strategy.

Back to the worms. So your friends say, "Look—you can just take a sliver of that worm to satisfy the cook, and then you can have all of these other wonderful foods that look delicious to you!" But, remember: no worm, no food... and you will go to bed hungry. When you keep the expectations small, (just a sliver), you are making the goal realistic. Over time, the portions can get larger, but the trick is to increase the portion size in a timeframe that's comfortable for you.

Let's return to reality and play this out in your own home. Let's say that the food you are trying to get them to eat is spinach. Although most parents won't have to drag the process on for so long, these are the steps for the most extreme of our picky eaters. Try each step for each meal until the fear begins to subside. It may take you days, weeks, or possibly months to get to normal portioning, but with patience, any child will progress. Remember, we are in it for the long haul, and for our child's healthy future!

Step 1: Touch the food. (Keep it to just one small spinach leaf.)
Step 2: Hold the spinach to the child's lips.
Step 3: Put the spinach leaf in the mouth, but do not swallow.
Step 4: Swallow whatever portion is in the mouth.
Step 5: Gradually increase the portion size.

For many children, just allowing the food on the same plate is a huge accomplishment. Take your time with this. It's essential to build the trust that you mean what you say, and that you will ask for nothing more. Refrain from saying, "Oh, you did such a great job, how about another bite?" That was not the agreement. The agreement needs to be made very clear. "Okay, Sara, all you have to do is put this in your mouth, then you can spit it out." When Sara does that, give a huge amount of praise, offer the reward of the food she wants, and DO NOT ask for more. By sticking to your end of the bargain, you are building trust and self-esteem.

The Gagger

I have heard from many parents who say the new foods they are trying to introduce will make their child throw up. This is why I stress the importance of a biomedical evaluation in the first chapter. Swallowing disorders are the main cause of gagging, however, for some children; self-induced vomiting is likely a fear-based response followed by the reward of not having to eat the offensive food. If your child is a gagger, and you have ruled out biomedical issues, overreaction on your part is strongly discouraged. The theory of keeping bites small in order to desensitize the child's reaction is your greatest defense. You may have to finely cut up all the challenging foods or liquefy them at first. This is not done with the intent to disguise the food as a long-term strategy. Work with the child to present the food in a texture they may enjoy, and if they say they cannot swallow, then puree or liquefy it. This works especially well for children with low cognitive abilities. Many parents will report that their child has a swallowing disorder, and I am always cautious and sympathetic to that, but when I ask what they eat, the parents cite a menu of chicken nuggets, French fries, crackers, and fruit snacks—all of which have complex textures. If those foods can be swallowed, the "disorder" may simply be fear.

If your child is struggling with texture sensitivities, here are some easy textures to get started. (Note: This is not the order I recommend for babies, as some of these foods are only appropriate for children who have enough teeth that they are able to chew well without risk of choking.)

Texture Type	Texture Description	Example
Smooth	Completely Smooth	Organic Baby Food
	Not Pureed	Acorn Squash, Mashed Sweet Potatoes, Mashed White Potatoes
Soft & Moist Solids	Ripe Fruit	Bananas, Papaya, Kiwi, Orange Segments, Seedless Grapes
	Well-Cooked Veggies	Green Beans, Broccoli, Zucchini, Spinach
	Grains	Small Varieties of Pasta, Rice, Oatmeal
Crunchy & Crumbly	Foods That Crunch And Fall Apart With Little Chewing Effort	Crackers, Toast, Breadsticks

How to Work with Children That Are Texture Sensitive

When Joey was little, trying to get him to eat a vegetable was "Mission Impossible." Because I knew he couldn't grow and heal his gut issues without a better diet, I devised the following strategy to get him to eat. Each child is so unique, you've got to experiment until you hit the right combination of texture and taste. Once you get them started, you can gradually introduce new elements.

Joey liked broth, so I knew that a smooth texture was the easiest place to start. I began with a basic bone broth recipe that I got from my friend and colleague Sueson Ross Vess.

Chicken Bone Broth

(May substitute turkey in place of chicken.)

Ingredients:

3 to 3 1/2 pounds free-range chicken pieces, mostly backs and wings, rinsed (Do not use the chicken liver, but you may use the giblets.)

2 carrots, cut in large chunks

3 celery stalks, cut in large chunks

2 large white onions, quartered

1 leek, rinsed and cut in large chunks

1 bay leaf

Handful of parsley and/or thyme sprigs (fresh)

1/2 teaspoon whole black peppercorns

1/2 teaspoon whole cloves

Cold, purified water

2 tablespoons vinegar or fresh lemon juice

Salt

Optional:

3-4 dried juniper berries (available at Penzeys Spices: www.penzeys.com or many grocery spice sections)

Place the chicken and vegetables in a large stockpot over medium heat. Pour enough cold water to cover chicken. Add vinegar or lemon juice. Add bay leaf, parsley/thyme, peppercorns, and cloves and slowly bring to a boil.
Lower the heat to medium-low and gently simmer for 3-4 hours uncovered (8 hours in a crock pot). The longer the stock cooks, the more flavorful and nutrient-dense the final result. As the broth cooks, skim any impurities that rise

to the surface; add a little more water if necessary to keep the chicken covered (when first simmering). It is normal to have some evaporation during cooking. If too much evaporation occurs, partially cover pan.

Remove the chicken pieces and discard. Strain the broth through a fine sieve into another pot to remove the vegetable solids. If not using the broth immediately, place the pot in a sink full of ice water and stir to cool. When cool, cover and refrigerate or freeze in portions that are easy to use. Broth will keep in the refrigerator for 3-4 days; freeze for extended use. Yield: 2 quarts

I would fill glass jars with the broth. Each day I would take out a quart of broth, steam a vegetable in the broth, and then puree it. I found that using the stems of kale in addition to the green leaves gave it a milky texture. I added plenty of sea salt, and made sure to get some of the broth fat in the soup. The first time I approached Joey with this, I was met with the usual resistance, but one day while Joey's dad was giving him a bath, I brought the soup into the bathroom. Joey was happiest at bath time and because he was usually sensory defensive, the bath helped relax and calm him. Very softly, I approached him with the soup and fed him a small bite full. He didn't spit it out, and I could tell he wanted more. Soon bath time became our nightly soup time. I didn't mind feeding him, and he loved the routine of it. I made medium to thick purees out of chicken, carrots, spinach, kale, butternut squash, and broccoli.

Altering Texture to Get Your Child to Eat Nutritious Foods

I'll never forget the day that I found my son Joey eating dry dog food. At the time, he was only eating cereal and crackers. I had just started taking his eating disorder seriously. Dry dog food? The food I was pushing him to eat must taste better than that, I thought. But strangely enough, he liked the texture and the crunch. This is when I realized that taste had little to do with his food preferences. Instead of focusing on taste, my new strategy was to create healthy foods that mimicked the same texture of cereal, crackers, and sadly, dog food. I had to make everything feel like that in his mouth. The theory actually worked. I used to bake crackers with vegetables in them. This recipe was my staple for Joey for four years. Although the cracker is great for all children who love crunchy texture, I invented it as a way for him to get the nutrition needed with his extreme food hypersensitivities. I would also pound meat until it was thin, bread it, and fry it until it was crisp.

Joey actually loved two textures—crispy and smooth. Because he lacked communication skills, I had to be realistic in my expectations, and therefore I needed to accommodate him more than I would have been willing to do with my other children. But I was more than willing to alter the healthy foods I was feeding him, always keeping in mind the two extremes of crunchy and smooth.

Food Texture Progression

"What's for dinner?" your child asks.

"Roasted chicken," you cheerfully reply.

"I don't like chicken," he insists.

"Yes, you do, you eat chicken nuggets all the time," you remind him.

"That's different," he concludes. "I'm not eating chicken!"

Who's right? How different is a chicken nugget from a piece of roasted chicken? The answer is, "Extremely" to a child with sensory issues. The good news is that if your child is eating chicken nuggets, you have the foundation to introduce a wider variety of foods. The concept is simple: Begin with the food they are eating, and gradually alter it until it becomes the food you desire them to eat. When I first had to take dairy away from my milk-guzzling daughter, I started by mixing cows milk and almond milk together to gradually get her used to the new flavor. I did the same thing when I switched from peanut butter to almond butter.

Here are some examples of food progression goals:

Food Progression Chart			
Eats Now	**Move To**	**Move To**	**Goal Food**
Chicken Nuggets	Chicken nuggets made with chunks of chicken instead of processed chicken	Fried whole pieces of chicken	Baked whole pieces of chicken
Cracker or Anything Crispy	Take thin and tender cuts of beef and pound them with a meat-tenderizing mallet until so thin, you can see light coming through. Dip in egg, then bread with breadcrumbs and lightly fry until crispy	Bread a thin steak and fry (Sometimes known as chicken fried steak)	Steak or any whole piece of meat
French Fries	Fried potato wedges	Baked potato wedges	Baked potato
Pureed Baby Food or Soup	Soup with small chunks of vegetables	Increase the size of vegetables	Sautéed vegetables
Apple Sauce	Sauce with small chunks of apples	Increase the size of the apple chunks	Diced fruit
Toast	French toast	French toast without syrup	Scrambled eggs

Help with Creamy, Smooth, and Crunchy Textures

Creamy Foods and Dips

- Pureed soup
- Pureed meats and vegetables (Similar to baby food)
- Indian Dal
- Creamy bean or lentil soups
- Mashed potatoes with mashed cooked cauliflower
- Smoothies
- Nut butters

  (Don't just think peanut: almond, cashew, macadamia, pecan, hazelnut, pumpkin seed, and sunflower seeds make wonderful options.)
- Refried beans
- Cream of rice, wheat, or buckwheat
- Oatmeal (You can take out some of the texture by putting the oats in the food processor first.)

- Smooth dips (Many wonderful healthy dips are found in Middle Eastern cookbooks.)
- Ketchup (Make sure it does NOT have high fructose corn syrup)
- Blended vegetables into ketchup
- Hummus
- Yogurt dips (You can make wonderful vegetable dips using plain yogurt.)
- Olive, pumpkin, and walnut oil (fresh and extra virgin) for dipping bread
- Roasted vegetable dips (Nightshade vegetables like eggplant, peppers, and tomatoes make wonderful pureed dips.)
- Guacamole
- Honey mustard (Made with local raw honey)
- Peanut Satay sauce

Crunchy Food

- Fried meat (Use tender cuts and pound until thin. Coat with egg, and then roll in breadcrumbs and fry.)
- Fried chicken nuggets (There are many recipes for chicken nuggets, but it's important for the picky eater that you use ground chicken or put whole pieces of chicken in the food processor where you pulse the meat until it breaks up, but is not pasty. Children with textures sensitivities will enjoy the chicken "falling apart in their mouth" feeling rather than needing to bite and chew.)

- Fried fish (Once again, it may help to put fish in the food processor first [pulse lightly] so that you are forming more of a crab cake look and feel, rather than a whole piece of fish.)
- Tempura vegetables
- Papadums (Bean flours fried or baked into crackers – available at Indian grocery stores.)
- Crispy tortillas or Pita bread (Best if baked or fried at home with good oil and served with healthy dip.)

Baked Crunchy Kale recipe

Kale and Brussels sprouts are a delicious crunchy treat when prepared using the following recipe:

1 whole head of flat leaf kale

1/4 cup of olive oil

Salt

Preheat oven to 325°. Wash and dry kale so that the water is no longer on the surface of the leaves. Lay kale down on a cutting board. With a paring knife, cut out the stem, leaving only the dark green leaves. Dip hands in olive oil and rub generously on the leaves. (For Brussels sprouts, peel off the outer leaves and coat with olive oil.)

Place leaves on a baking sheet. Generously salt. Place in oven. Cooking time will vary depending on the size and thickness of leaves. When they are crunchy, the kale will turn dark green and the sprouts will turn a light brown. Remove from oven before they turn dark brown. They should crunch. If they turn soft, return them to oven for a r more minutes. One head of kale makes enough for a ramily snack. If they get soggy, just throw them back in the oven for a couple of minutes to get rid of the moisture.

Here are some creative venues for adding nutrition for texture-sensitive picky eaters:

- Meatloaf (Add pureed vegetables)
- Mashed potatoes (Add mashed cauliflower, parsnip, rutabaga, or jimaca)
- Pasta sauce (Add pureed vegetables: tomatoes are great at masking flavors that are unique)
- Smoothies (Throw in carrots, green vegetables, seeds, or nuts)
- Baked goods (Replace water or milk with pureed steamed vegetables)
- Quesadillas (Add spinach leaves, avocado, peppers, or fresh tomatoes)

Healthy Servings of Protein and Vegetables

We live in a time when strawberries are available year round, and you can buy a banana at a gas station. Today "food" is abundant and cheap—thanks to the production and shipping methods of giant food companies. As consumers, we demand lower and lower prices at the grocery store, not realizing the true cost that our bodies are paying. What ends up on the shelves, however, bears little resemblance to its original counterpart in nature, and does little or nothing to feed our bodies or our souls. But even though truly nutritional food may not be available at every gas station, eating well doesn't have to be hard. You don't need to read every article and over analyze every new government report. Ignore the Food Pyramid because it's not relevant. Just eat a variety of REAL food. That's it. When I say "real food," I am talking about food that is not overly preserved, processed, or packaged to the point that you need special tools to open it. I have seen children in Costa Rica who are considered "poor" eating rice, beans, and indigenous fruits and vegetables, and they have a healthier diet than many American children.

I was taking a walk with a man in Costa Rica years back who told me stories about his boyhood, and how he and his friends would steal mangos from the trees. I told him, "Well, that wouldn't happen in America."

He asked, "Oh—American children don't steal?"

"No," I said, "They don't eat mangos."

At the very minimum, your children should get two servings of vegetables a day, and by servings, I mean a half a cup for little ones and a full cup for those who have reached puberty. I would not count corn or white potato products in these servings, as they fall more into the starch category. Although there are health benefits to organic corn and white potatotes, they don't take the place of low glycemic and nutritionally dense sweet potatoes and yams. Ideally, the best time to get vegetables in our children is breakfast, but that might be a challenge you are not up for in the morning. What I recommend for parents who really need quick and easy to get everyone out the door is to have kids eat sprouts. Sunflower, alfalfa, bean, whatever you can easily find at your local grocery store. Sprouts don't have a strong flavor, they are best if they are eaten raw, and they are fast and fun to eat. I used to give them to my kids with their vitamins. It was not made into a big deal, so it was never an issue for them, and they liked the taste. The best way to introduce a new food concept is to keep it very low-key. If you have a lot of anxiety or expectation, you can bet that your children will pick up on that in a heartbeat. Start small, have fun with it (you can all pretend to be bunnies!), and eventually move into a handful to satisfy their metabolic needs.

An even better option for the "advanced nutritional" crowd is cultured vegetables. These great jar vegetables are available at health food stores, but are simple and inexpensive to make at home. They provide probiotics, digestive enzymes, B vitamins, and more. They are one of the recommended foods from the Weston A. Price Foundation, and you can get recipes or more information by going to their website at www.westonaprice.org.

My kids love to tell the story of the rare occasions that John would stop at the bakery on the way home from work and buy bread and donuts. In the morning, the kids would come down to breakfast only to find the donut on a plate accompanied by a small bowl of cultured vegetables. The moaning and groaning…"Way to ruin a meal, Mom," didn't stop them from eating the cultured vegetables so they could enjoy their bakery treats.

As for protein, three times a day is my recommendation. A quick and easy way to measure a serving is to visualize a rounded amount (like a small ball) of the protein in the eater's hand. Little hands need smaller amounts. America has been trained to wake up each morning and throw the emptiest of nutritional foods into our bodies: pastries, sugar cereal (I don't care how fortified it is, as most of them use junky vitamins that can't be absorbed by the body), Pop tarts, or the top shelf expensive "pop strudels"…Yes, those marketing people really know their stuff!

High protein foods such as meats, poultry, eggs, fish, beans, nuts, seeds, and some "grain-like" foods like quinoa and oats (in whole form – not pulverized and mixed with mini marshmallows), need to be eaten in handful sizes three times a day.

Motivation: First This, Then That!

The behavioral approach of "First This, Then That" is taught to children with autism who are in Applied Behavior Analysis (ABA) therapy. I watched therapists do this for years with my son, until finally I realized "First This, Then That" was the ideal approach to entice children to eat unfamiliar foods. As in ABA, when you want a certain behavior, you have to adequately motivate the child, and make the reward accessible and achievable.

When I work with a new parent, I customize where to begin based on the cognitive ability of the child, therefore, in teaching this to you, we will start at the most extreme of sensory defensiveness and move our way into strategies for the adolescent child or teenager. Please note that I only use examples of the desired food that you wish your child to eat and the food that is used as the motivator. You should use whatever combination of foods works for your child.

Severe Sensory Defensiveness

The child has little understanding of your verbal request, is extremely sensitive to almost all textures, and will not touch unfamiliar food.

Goal: Touching the food

Process: Allow the child to play with the food. Let him get familiar with the texture by holding it. Make the piece of food extremely small (approximately the size of their fingernail). If the child does not want to hold the food, then take an item the child loves to eat. If it's a chip, say, "First hamburger, than chip." Give the child a small piece of chip each time they touch the hamburger. Continue with this until you feel the child is comfortable with touching the hamburger. This may take days, as you don't want to make the child scared and uncomfortable. If you are not getting cooperation, DO NOT GIVE THEM THE CHIP. You can offer something else to eat, but the chip at this point has changed from potato to tool. You need to be consistent, and bring the little piece of hamburger and chip with you to the playroom, the park, Grandma's, or wherever the child feels comfortable. Celebrate enthusiastically when you achieve this goal!

Moderately Severe Sensory Defensiveness

Little understanding of verbal requests, is extremely sensitive to almost all textures, will touch food, but will not eat.

Goal: Getting the food in the mouth and chewed

Process: This is a three-part process. The first step is to get the child to put the food to his lips, the second is to get the child to put the food in his mouth, and the third is to chew the food. The process is similar to what is explained in extreme sensory defensiveness.

So, it's "First chicken, then cracker," and model how the child needs to hold the piece of chicken to the lips. Again, the piece of food can be very small. Once the child is comfortable, you can progress to having them put the chicken in his/her mouth. Once again, model how this is done. It is very easy to get frustrated, as it may not seem like you are asking for much, but the calmer you stay, the more likely your child will cooperate. If you scare or force the child in any way, he will not trust that this will be a pleasant experience, and will be resistant. He can spit out the food, or simply place the food on the tongue, and then remove it. The next step is to get him to chew the food. He can still spit it out, but he has to chew it. For the child with more severe sensory issues, serve only pureed foods, and allow the chewing step to be skipped. Celebrate enthusiastically when you achieve this goal!

Moderate Sensory Defensiveness

Sensitive to textures, will allow food in the mouth, but will not swallow.

Goal: Swallowing the food

Process I (For children limited in understanding verbal requests): Once again, the piece of food should be about the size of a fingernail. This time, I would have a larger portion of something your child really does like. You can use liquid, like juice for your reinforcing food, but always offer water to the child. Never withhold water.

Say to the child, "First carrot, then juice." (If the child is non-verbal, and only used to spitting out the food at this point, it can be tricky teaching him that now he has to swallow the food. This is why liquid works well for this process. Model what you mean by swallowing, and then, when the food is in the mouth, have the child take a sip of juice. (Many children will naturally swallow the carrot with the juice, but make sure the carrot is chewed or already pureed before allowing a sip of juice.) Once again, do not give the reinforcing food (in this case, juice) unless the child swallows. Celebrate enthusiastically when you achieve this goal!

Process II (For children with a full understanding of verbal requests): For many of you, this is where you will begin "First This, Then That." This method is for the child who completely understands what you are asking of her, but refuses to participate. This process needs to begin with a conversation. Let her know that you are going to expect her to try new foods because you love her so much and you love her body and want to keep it healthy and strong. She is still going to get to eat some of her favorite foods, but she is going to first have to try small bites of other foods. The purpose of having this conversation before the actual event is to give her some time to process the request. You don't want to catch her by surprise when it's time to introduce the new food. The next time the child is hungry is a great time to begin. The following is an example of a conversation between you and your child.

Child: "I'm hungry."

Parent: "Great! Remember what we talked about? You have to have a 'special bite' of the new food."

Child: "I don't want to do that now. I just want some crackers."

Parent: "I bet you really would like some crackers, but first I want you to try one-half of this little tiny blueberry. I'm going to slice a tiny piece for you to try."

Child: "No way. I'm not trying it. I won't eat anything."

Parent: "Okay, let me know when you are ready."

One hour goes by:

Child: "I want a glass of juice!"

Parent: "Sure, I would love to pour that for you, but first, you need to try half of that blueberry."

Child: (Crying) "You are so mean!"

Parent: "I love you enough to know that I want you healthy, and that means eating food that is good for you."

Child: "I won't try it."

Parent: "Okay, here's a glass of water. That should quench your thirst."

Dinnertime:

Parent: "Wow, you must be hungry."

Child: "I'm starving and you're trying to kill me!" (I've heard accusations like that and worse from some of the parents I have worked with on picky eating.)

Parent: "I know this is new to you and you are scared. Let's think of ways we can make it easier to eat that blueberry. Maybe we can dip it into something or mash it into something."

Child: "Like what?"

Parent: "How about if I watch you mash it into a little glass, and then you can pour a tiny bit of juice into the glass and drink it really fast?"

Child: (Sullenly) "Okay, I guess."

Here are some other ideas for working with different types of foods:

Hamburger

Parent: "How about if we get your favorite ketchup, and draw a truck with the ketchup on your plate and make the hamburger the wheel? You can get the hamburger so covered up in ketchup that you don't even see the brown color." (Always use non-HFCS ketchup.)

Broccoli

Parent: "Why don't you mash up that broccoli and then mix it into your mashed potatoes?" (Don't do too many potatoes, as they may not finish them all.) Or introduce the broccoli to the French fry:

Parent: "Look! The broccoli and the French fry are the same size. I think they could be great friends and you can chew them up together!"

The most important rule with all of these techniques is that you must keep the rule going until the child has tried the food. Ask your doctor how comfortable he/she is about your child refusing food for a day as you take on this challenge. Most will say that if the child is getting water, she can go a couple of days without food, although few children will hold out longer than an evening. Going to bed hungry may be necessary to make your point. If you are concerned about them getting other foods at school, start the process on a Friday night.

Once successful with this method, aim to introduce something new once a day. Keep it small and achievable. In time, make the "Special Bite" (that's a great name to call it) be a part of every meal. Then gradually increase the size of the "Special Bite" so that it is a standard, chewable size. Remember: Celebrate enthusiastically when you achieve this goal!

Mild Sensory Defensiveness

Has eaten meat or vegetables before, just really dislikes them.

Goal: Three bites

Process: Every meal requires three bites of something nutritious. The less drama you attach to this, the better. Don't argue, don't negotiate, just be firm on your intention and don't back down. Each time you back down, you teach the child that they simply need to whine or fight you a little bit more to get their desired outcome. This is tough love at its best. You are not doing this to "get your way," you are doing this purely out of love. My daughters really appreciate their love of food now, but they didn't appreciate the "three bite" rule when they were first introduced to new foods. Remember the long-term result you are working for when you feel frustrated or discouraged. Getting them to eat a healthy diet is worth the struggle!

At this stage, I allow the children to eat other foods in between each "Special Bite," but make sure the three bites are finished before the child gets full. They can dip, smash, hide, or cut; don't put any restrictions on their creative ways to eat it.

Very Mild Sensory Defensiveness

Eats three bites, but that's it.

Goal: Eat a serving (a serving is about the size of the palm of their hand rounded.)

Process: Rotate between the "Special Bite" food and the food they enjoy. They are welcome to finish the meat or vegetable first, but many children feel more comfortable rotating back and forth with bites. I'm always sharing the story of my children rotating cultured vegetables and donuts for breakfast with my clients!

Case Study: When Your Child Won't Eat

Bryce was one of my more challenging picky eaters. At the age of five, he was exceptionally thin, and at one point completely stopped eating. His parents would have been thrilled to see him even eat a piece of candy, much less anything healthy. Bryce was extremely sick, and everyone agreed that some heavy duty medical testing was necessary: liver and kidney function, blood count, and stool (if possible). There are many possibilities when a child stops eating, but it is important that you understand the distinction of "not eating" as some parents may call it, even though they are referring to a picky eater who doesn't eat much, and "not eating" as it applies to a child who truly doesn't eat anything at all and is at risk.

At this point, all that was in my diet counseling bag of tricks was out the window, as Bryce was essentially starving himself. There was no, "First This, Then That"... because there was no "That." He did drink water, and mom would give him baking soda baths because he would drink the water in the bathtub. He had not eaten a morsel in four days, and my husband, Dr. Hicks, recommended that Bryce be evaluated for a feeding tube.

The next day an X-ray showed impacted stool throughout the colon. Pediatric Fleet enemas were given, and Bryce's appetite started to return. From the intake history, we subsequently found out the child had been exceptionally constipated because his diet consisted totally of dairy and simple carbs. The lack of fiber in his diet forced a tremendous backup in his colon that stopped his appetite. I worked with the parents on a high fiber diet, and because they had been through such a scare, they were now very mindful of what Bryce ate. Within a week the feeding tube was removed, and Bryce was getting color back in his cheeks.

One year later, the family came to visit. I could hardly believe my eyes, as Bryce was now a strong and bright little boy. Mom said he ate better than they did, and although she still has nightmares of his hospitalization, she is grateful for the experience, because she now understands the value of a well-rounded diet.

Motivation Strategies by Age Group

Babies

If you are fortunate enough to get these tips before you have introduced your baby to solids, then your road will be much easier. Sadly, instead of opening the door to the wonderful world of food when babies start eating solids, well-meaning parents slam it shut, never realizing that they are setting the stage for picky eating and potential life-long health problems. Most picky eating begins between the ages of one and two. Although I understand that parents mean no harm, when I see a baby being given a French fry or a bottle of juice, I cringe at the prospect of a classic "Picky Eater" set up.

The best foundation for a breast-fed baby's healthy relationship to food is a mother who eats a well-rounded and healthy diet that is not too weighted by simple carbs. Breast-feeding introduces a variety of foods to the baby's diet, and it's important to remember that if you eat organic, so does your baby! Many babies will act negatively to breast milk when the mother is eating certain foods.

If your child is colicky, mom's diet should be evaluated to find the source of the trigger food(s). Some of the most common culprits are dairy, gluten, and soy. Doing an elimination diet can help highlight which foods may be triggering reactions in the colicky baby.

Babies do not need juice! In fact, the longer you can hold off from anything sweet, the better. Pureed orange vegetables are a great place to start, moving into pureed meats and rice, then to green vegetables, and finally to fruits that are unsweetened. After nursing or formula, introducing as much water as possible not only keeps your little one hydrated, it will prevent "Juice Belly"—the overly full tummy loaded with the fructose found in most juices. Babies that are big juice drinkers not only have a huge increase in dental problems, but also learn that every liquid needs to be sweet. Many juice drinkers as babies become soda drinkers as adults.

As babies grow into toddlers, encourage their discovery of new foods by allowing them to get messy. Babies clean well and so do bibs! The baby that grows into a toddler with the freedom to "play with his/her food" will be much more comfortable with every new food experience. Fun takes the fear out of food.

Toddlers to Pre-Schoolers

Doctors will say it's "normal" for toddlers to become picky because they are beginning to discover their independence. Allowing them to assert their new freedom and sense of self does not mean that you give up power at the dinner table. The two don't have to go hand in hand. By all means give them a choice, "Do you want spinach or carrots?" The problems start when parents give up all control over the menu. You can't ask a two year old, "Do you want spinach or crackers?" Or even worse, "Do you want any green beans?" It's frustrating to hear the litany of wheedling, open-ended questions paraded before the willful toddler by today's parents. Directing toddlers while still giving them clear choices is a wonderful way to keep meal-time positive, and helps you set clear boundaries in healthy food options.

Another concern I have is overfeeding toddlers. My Italian grandmother loved to feed me. She made all my favorite foods, but I remember knowing that there were no other options—what was in front of me was the meal. Naturally, I ate and enjoyed it… but if I had turned up my nose at spaghetti… she wasn't about to whip up some mashed potatoes just for me.

I also find that many parents get nervous if their child is not eating as much this week as they did last week. As adults, we all go through cyclical changes in our levels of hunger. How many times have you remarked, "I don't know what it is—but I have been so hungry all day!" If today's breakfast is scrambled eggs, and they pick at them lightly, then assume they are full and put the eggs away in a container. If they are hungry 15 minutes later, bring back the eggs, but don't make French toast. This is how clever little children begin turning their parents into short order cooks.

Introduce flavor right from the start. The easiest way to get wonderful antioxidants down our children at an early age without adding a variety of textures is to introduce as many herbs and spices as possible. All of these flavors are an acquired taste, and because they provide so much nutrition, they are smart ingredients to add wherever you can. If you are pureeing chicken for your 18 month old, add some basil. If you are pureeing sweet potatoes, add some turmeric and ginger. It is true that babies have more taste buds than we do as adults, but light amounts of flavor create a palate that is acceptable to both taste and smell.

Here's an example of a meal plan for a healthy two-year old eater like my nephew Ronan:

Breakfast

Protein is vital to satisfying hunger at any age. Make sure to provide some form of protein, fiber, and vitamin dense foods—preferably a vegetable, but a piece of fruit is okay. Here are some examples:

- Scrambled eggs cooked in butter or olive oil (Sprinkle in chopped parsley.)
- Oatmeal with raisins (For children over two, add nuts.)
- Plain whole milk yogurt sweetened with fresh fruit (For children over two, add small amounts of local raw honey.)
- Whole grain toast with butter
- Chicken or turkey sausage

Snacks

Two snacks should be given each day centered between breakfast and lunch, and lunch and dinner. The first snack of the day is usually a busy time for little ones. Parents know that this is usually their happiest time, and often the best time for errands. Healthy food that can be packed on the go is important for this snack.

- Cut-up fruit
- Nuts and seeds (For children over the age of two)
- Fresh peas
- Vegetable chunks in safe-to-eat sizes
- Hard-boiled egg
- Meat chunks (Make the pieces small enough for easy grabbing and eating.)
- Smoothies made with a variety of vegetables and fruit

Lunch

- Soups (Egg drop, bean soup, chicken or beef soups with whole chunks or pureed vegetables)
- Pasta (Small noodles) Delicious with tomato sauces, olive oil or butter, and curry sauces with vegetables pureed into the sauce
- Fresh vegetables with hummus or other type of bean dip
- Whole grain bread sandwiches focusing more on meat than cheese

Dinner

Here are some sample meals the whole family will love and the food can be easily chopped up in smaller bites for little ones:

- Roasted meats, sweet potatoes, steamed vegetables with olive oil or butter
- Baked chicken (skin left on), rice, and stir fried vegetables
- Fresh fish pan-fried, poached, or sautéed with olive oil and butter with fresh vegetables and potatoes
- Dessert: Fruit in season

Junior High and High School: Coping with the Picky Eating Teenager

Of my three children, Mia is my "foodie." Since she was a little girl, she loved flavor. Because I wasn't a fantastic cook back then, she was frequently disappointed, but exceptionally enthusiastic when something went right. She was picky, but thinking back, she was just picky about good quality food. She hated McDonalds, but loved cabbage soup. One of her favorite foods was salad, and she still loves her salad. Because of a few developmental delays, I put Mia on a gluten and casein free diet when she was seven years old, and it was beneficial. She was a trouper with all of the changes, as my other two children were much younger when I converted their diets, and Jessie, her younger sister, went right from breast milk to rice milk. Mia started first grade right after I started her on the diet. Naturally, on the first day of school, I sent her off with her favorite salad with all kinds of chopped vegetables, sunflower seeds, and French dressing.

She came home from school on the first day and quickly told me she was pretty sure salads were not allowed in the school.

I questioned why. She went on to tell me that none of the other children had salad, and most of them looked very strangely at hers. I assured her that salads were allowed, and let her teacher know to mention this to her. Children want to fit in.

My daughter Jessie is much more attuned to "feeling different." She wouldn't let me send special treats for her the days the other kids were eating food that I wouldn't allow. She would rather pass on the sugary treat than bring something strange from home. I know there are many parents who wish schools would do more to keep chemical and preservative-laden foods off the lunch menu, although some private schools have done a great deal to support healthy eating. Schools also know that kids' test scores improve, and behaviors are more cooperative, when children refrain from junk foods.

Both of my daughters have been blessed with an amazing "Home Living" middle school teacher. Mrs. Blakely has done an outstanding job of helping the children understand the dangers of high fructose corn syrup and chemicals in foods.

I am well aware that teenagers are not going to play fun little eating games and they certainly are much more innovative about finding free junk food. However, it also does not mean that you need to give up if your child has soared through adolescence on French fries and Mountain Dew, with no intention of changing his/her diet now.

The self-esteem of teenagers is so fragile that you want to assure them that they aren't being "punished" because they look "fat" or "scrawny." I have had many teenagers say to me that the only reason anyone would watch their diet is if they had a weight problem. Doing it for better health and a longer life is NOT going to motivate most teenagers who live for the day. Our teens are getting extremely mixed advice from the media. They are being told all fats are bad, and many develop hormonal problems because they avoid any type of fat at all cost. Without healthy fats, our cells are not flexible. Our brains require healthy fats to function properly—and today's teenage sensory-soaked brains need all the help they can get!

Many teens also experience acne that can be dramatically improved with a more wholesome diet that includes healthy fats, low glycemic and complex carbs, and mineral rich foods, especially zinc. Their need for focus and concentration increases as school becomes more intense and fatigue frequently sets in during the late teen years as the body can no longer function properly without the proper amount of amino acids, vitamins, minerals, and, again, healthy fats.

But how do you get your teen to care? Begging, pleading, and especially threatening usually diminish any listening power you possibly already had. The best course of action is to live by example. As long as all grocery-purchasing adults are on the same team, then you can have a say as to what they eat in the house.

Interview with Middle School Kids

The subject of picky eating is not limited to parents and professionals. Kids have their own opinions on picky eating, and they can be quite revealing. I interviewed seven 12 and 13 year-old middle school girls who are in my daughter Jessie's seventh grade class. Before we started, I made sure everyone understood that there were no right or wrong answers.

I asked the girls to give me their definition of a picky eater. They all had very clear views, and described it best as only wanting some foods and not others. Then I asked the "picky eaters" to identify themselves. Both Ashley and Cherri raised their hands, but the girls all looked at Ashley and would have identified her even if she hadn't.

Betsy: "For those of you who do consider yourselves picky eaters, do you think it's okay to be a picky eater?"

Ashley: "Not really, because I feel I make people mad or sad when my grandparents make something for me and I don't like it."

Cherri: "My mom makes really healthy food, but sometimes

I'm just picky because I only want what I feel like eating."

Betsy: "That seems fair, but I made all of you Hungarian Goulash for breakfast. And you all ate it. That must have seemed strange."

Cherri: "Yeah, but it was good."

Yvanna: "That's really it. Healthy food is great to eat when it tastes good."

Betsy: "So if foods like that Goulash or fresh salads or roasted nuts were waiting for you when you come home from school, would you still reach for the chips?"

Ashley: "I would like to eat healthy, but growing up in a house where no one is even trying to eat healthy makes it hard to have good things to eat. They will say things to me like, 'You need to lose weight,' but they don't buy me the food to help me lose weight."

Yvanna: "Yeah, healthy food is expensive."

Ashley: "It is, and I'm a kid, I don't have money. I need them to buy it for me and healthy food is expensive."

Betsy: "Actually, it's not so much that healthy food is expensive as much as fake food is cheap."

Cherri: "Definitely, it costs a lot more to eat lots of fresh stuff. I love fresh stuff and the worst place for that is the school. I would totally eat more healthy food at the school if they had it."

Betsy: "But they say the opposite. They say that they try giving you healthy options, and it goes to waste because no one eats it."

Ashley: "But nothing is fresh, the watermelon is mushy."

Cherri: "And the peppers are browning."

Chey: "And the grapes are kind of smooshed."

Yvanna: "And the fruit all sits together so it all tastes the same. The apples taste like oranges, the oranges taste like bananas."

Chey: "The pizza, when you hold it up, the grease drips off of it."

Jessie: "It's just so gross for you."

Yvanna: "And the sad part is we have a new girl in our class, and she said compared to her old school, our lunches were good."

Betsy: "Okay, let's talk about your parents. Cherri, you told me your dad is a picky eater."

Cherri: "He is a really picky eater. I wouldn't even call him a picky eater because that's too nice of a term. My mom makes all kinds of meats and vegetables and he won't eat most of it. She'll make something [good] and he'll throw something junky in the microwave."

Michelle: "My mom, she won't eat anything unless it has corn it in. Everything has to have corn."

Betsy: "Tell me about when you are all older and buying your own groceries. Will you still eat vegetables?"

Cherri, Yvanna, Hannah: "Yeah, we'll eat vegetables and make home cooked meals."

Ashley: "Yes, but sometimes we'll be in a hurry, so I probably won't always be able to eat healthy foods 'cause we'll have other responsibilities. It's okay to eat out every now and then."

Michelle and Chey: "Sometimes you have to rely on a boxed food."

Betsy: "Do you all think you'll eat vegetables when you have families?"

Cherri: "Yes, because I love the taste of vegetables."

Yvanna: "But money can be hard and sometimes I may not be able to afford them."

Hannah: "I'll eat vegetables, but not all the vegetables because there are some that I really don't like—like broccoli."

Ashley: "I think it will be easier because you can buy the vegetables that you like."

Betsy: "I talk in my book about strategies for getting teenagers to eat meat and vegetables that they don't like to eat. Let's say you really like French fries and your parents want you to try to eat some meat. So they tell you that you have to eat three bites of meat in order to get your fries. Do you think that is fair?"

Cherri: "Definitely. It's not hard to eat three bites. My parents do that now. I don't think it's really forcing, because it's still a choice. Kids don't have to eat it, but if they want something else, then they know what they have to do."

Ashley: "I think that's very fair."

Betsy: "What about if you have to eat three equal portions of vegetables, meat, and maybe a potato?"

Jessie: "I think it's good because it evens everything out."

Cherri: "I think it's good, because you won't get full on just one thing."

The girls loved talking about this subject and most who had been exposed to organic foods said they could taste the difference, and preferred organic over conventional produce.

The lessons I learned from this conversation reinforced so much of what I have believed and taught in my workshops and practice. Children do like healthy food when it's purchased, prepared, and presented well. I was saddened to hear so many of the girls talk about healthy food as a financial luxury. But it was interesting to hear Cherri relate the story of her father heating something "junky" in the microwave instead of eating the family dinner. The cost of that surely outweighs the cost of purchasing fresh food. Most girls had pizza regularly and ate out often. And once again, fresh healthy food that tastes great does not have to cost more than a meal out, even if it is fast food.

Bringing the joy of real food back to the table, and planting the desire in our children to embrace delicious and healthy food starts with great ingredients and cooking techniques. How wonderful it would be if schools would teach kids the real facts about food and nutrition, and how to make nourishing family meals instead of sugary treats and snacks!

Peer Pressure

My daughter Mia's 14 year-old friend came over for dinner one evening. As they were walking through the kitchen, her friend asked, "Hi, Mrs. Hicks, what's for dinner?"

"We're having salmon…" I began.

"Cool, I've never had salmon," she replied. That didn't surprise me, as many of my children's friends don't eat fish. I continued, "And we're having salad."

"I've never had a salad before," she said. (Did I mention she was 14?)

"Actually," I said slowly, preparing myself for her next comment, "we're having spinach salad."

"Spinach! Well I've never had that, but I heard about it on Sponge Bob," she said with enthusiasm.

She actually ate everything and loved it! It just goes to show that we don't always give our children credit for what they might try, especially when they are at someone's house and their friend and whole family is eating it.

How many times have we heard the parents of our children's friends mention things like, "You're so lucky that your daughter is helpful around the house. She offered to wash dishes and was the only girl who made her bed after the sleepover." And you stand there with your mouth open, wondering whom they are talking about, since the last time your daughter volunteered to be helpful she was still in diapers! The same thing is true for eating habits. Your picky eater may turn up his nose at green beans in your kitchen, but ask for seconds when faced with being the only one not eating them at his best friend's house.

Mia's Story

Written by Mia Prohaska, aged 16

When I was first introduced to a life where picky eating was not allowed, I was confused. I didn't understand why my diet of Reese's Pieces and French fries wouldn't suffice as healthy eating. However, this change would end up being one of the greatest gifts in my life. Little by little, I learned to love the leafy things my mom had put on my plate. Looking back as to why my perspective on eating changed so much, it was because eating became an adventure to me. It was like playing a new game, "What new flavor will I experience next? What new food will I learn to love?"

Food is meant to be an art—a way of expressing ourselves through unique flavors. So next time you get a choice between eating out at the local burger joint or an Arabian restaurant down the street, go for the new. Your child might not appreciate the new cuisine the first few times, but in the long run, they'll learn to love not only food, but also wonderful cultures. Food is a gift of life, and I learned that because of my wonderful mother who dared me to try something new.

Food and Kids: Society's Marketing Insanity

Humor me for a minute. I'd like to take you to an isolated island. For the sake of argument, the island teems with lush vegetation, has plenty of protein, and a temperate climate. In other words, natural sources of food abound. A family lives there, awaiting the birth of their child. They live simply, but well. Naturally, when the baby is born, she is breast-fed. There are no stores, so her birth is not heralded with toys, gimmicks, marketing barrages, or the truckload of cute supplies that every child supposedly can't live without.

As the months pass, she starts to try the family food, encouraged to experiment in whatever way she sees fit. She gnaws on a chicken leg. She sucks on an orange rind. She plays with the mashed sweet potatoes on her mother's plate. She grabs a chili pepper, pops it in her mouth, and makes a face. Her older brother imitates her, laughing. She does it again, and she laughs, too. She does not have a fancy bib, a high chair that plays music, Sesame Street tableware, or her own plastic dining set.

As she grows older, she will eat what the family eats, and learn how to find, clean, and prepare the food with her family. She will never know that there is an entire alternate universe of "children's foods"—"fake" food in the form of brightly colored snacks, cereal, and candy—full of artificial flavors, colors, additives, and preservatives, all packaged in bright, happy containers with prizes, games, fueled by endorsements and TV shows, kiddie celebrities and cartoon characters—enormous amounts of time, effort, and money dedicated to the sole purpose of getting kids to eat foods that are not good for them.

When you step back and look at the big picture of how we market food to children in our culture, it's insanity. When did we decide that kids wouldn't eat real food that tastes good? Instead of giving them delicious, nutritious food, we feed them junk on a brightly colored plate or in a special "Lunchable" package.

The food we feed children doesn't need to visually dazzle or dance on the plate; it just needs to taste good. Addictive preservatives, chemicals, and simple carb cravings set our children up to be junk food junkies. I am overjoyed when I see parents pureeing their healthy dinner for their baby, or parents who routinely expose their children to a variety of flavors. In parts of Asia, parents will touch a chili pepper to babies' lips to get them used to the spiciness of foods. Allowing children to dip hardy breads into olive oil with crushed garlic is a wonderful introduction to stronger flavors. For older toddlers, enjoying the multi-sensory experience of a chicken leg is part of the fun of learning about food. Share your food with your child, and don't assume they won't like it because it's not a "kid" food. And remember—if they don't like it the first time, keep trying. Some things, like beautifully steamed broccoli with organic butter and lemon, are worth fighting for!

Creative Food

Most families get into a rut with the same recipes and types of food night after night. It's no wonder that boredom often sets in, and children turn away at dinnertime. In this chapter, the focus is adding creativity to breakfasts, lunches, and dinners.

There are two possibilities for a definition of creative food. The food industry and marketing world would tell you that it's about adding color and zing to boring foods. That our children need to be dazzled in order to choose the right oatmeal, ketchup, drink, or candy. Sadly, they have done a disservice to our children by turning food into a vast chemical extravaganza. It's not hard to sell anything with cute kids, animation, and loads of artificial color and flavor—not to mention a billion dollar advertising budget.

The type of creative food I am speaking about is the "Food Network" version. It's the parsley on the plate, and the homemade sauce or gravy that dresses up the meat or fish. It's cutting radishes into flowers, and adding mint to your ice tea. It's NOT using artificial colored sugar to decorate your pancakes. Creative food is the part of cooking where the artist in you comes out to play.

I live in a rural area, where organic grocery and produce options are limited, and our restaurant choices fall somewhere between fast food chains and tavern fare. Although things have improved, I'm pretty sure that some places still consider vegetables with color to be ketchup, pickles, and anything under bright orange cheese sauce. Many people who live here don't expect or appreciate culinary innovation. That's why I'm always so happy when my daughter's friends come over and can enjoy a home cooked meal. How do they know that fresh, real food can taste so much better if they never get to try it? Maybe that's where you are too. Maybe you have grown up and lived your life in a town like this. In many ways, small town America is the greatest place in the world. I can't imagine a better place to raise my children than in the beauty of Wisconsin, along with my safe, kind, and loving community, but too many people eat what they know, and never try anything new. That's why I have such huge appreciation for the Food Network and other cooking shows! They introduced the world to recipes and foods that couldn't be appreciated or understood from a cookbook. You can go online now and find thousands of recipes for every cuisine imaginable, or search You Tube for private cooking classes in your kitchen whenever you feel like learning something new. I think back to my early experiments with Joey's special diet. Cooking and nutrition know-how has come a long way!

This chapter will help wake up the artistic genius in you that wants creative food, but doesn't know where to start.

Starting Off with Breakfast

Sweetened cereal is one of the most nutritiously void and gut-bacteria forming foods made. In the last few deades, it has caused many children to have morning stomachaches that keep them from going to school. Homemade oatmeal is not difficult to make, and the reason kids like the packaged kind is because of the excitotoxin additions.

However, the best breakfast you can serve is leftover dinner. Equipped with protein and vegetables, leftovers are a perfect start to the day. Organic eggs are extremely nutritious, as are turkey bacon and chicken sausage, but it will get boring if you eat it everyday. For the child who doesn't want to eat breakfast, frozen fruit smoothies with fresh bananas and a sprinkling of protein powder can be a perfect choice. This is great for the family where no one sits for breakfast. Smoothies can be slurped down while doing your hair and getting dressed.

My greatest concern for your breakfast choice is the acidity of most breakfast foods. This lack of alkalizing foods causes stomachaches, acid reflux, and digestive issues. However, if they choose a food without nutritional content, compromise by having them munch a few spinach leaves, eat a handful of sprouts, or even drink a cup of green tea (use quality tea made at 175 degrees). Alkaline foods like these will make a big difference for their growing bodies.

Looking Forward to Lunch

For many years, I packed lunches for my children. I had all of them on gluten and casein-free diets, so it was more of a necessity than a choice. When they were in elementary school, they were teased for bringing homemade meals, but once they hit about 7th grade, they were envied. I have found that children begin to appreciate home cooked meals much more in the teen years. They get tired of the same "kids foods" and they love the smells of fresh ingredients. Until that point hits, however, lunch can be a real struggle because you are not there to monitor their food choices. You can provide perfectly balanced meals, but it's hard to know what gets tossed and what gets traded at school. The circumstances certainly vary per child. My son had an aide with him at lunch, so his diet was strictly followed, and some of you may be blessed to have your children at a school where they actually serve "real food." I was in California recently and discovered a company called "Children's Choice" that caters organic lunches to schools throughout the state of California. What a wonderful resource for parents who are trying to ensure that their children have healthy choices for school lunches!

I honestly don't like to dictate lunch choices to parents and prefer they make their own decisions based on what feels right to them. I know many parents who barely make it through dinner, and if their child is getting one healthy meal a day, that's a great accomplishment. Hopefully some of you may have a bit more time to prepare meals. Maybe you are doing it out of necessity because of food allergies or intolerances. In those cases, keep the rules for dinner alive at lunch.

One trap that I urge you not to get in is the "Lunchable" plastic carton. Please don't succumb to that processed, non-nutritious, plastic coated, color-enhanced, and pre-packaged world. These fake foods are marketed during cartoons and sold to kids through clever brainwashing ads. The amount of money that is wasted and the garbage that is generated is truly purposeless.

Plan Ahead: Creating Dinners That Work

You don't have to have your meals look like a page from Bon Appétit magazine, but there are some simple tricks to putting meals together. Just like coordinating an outfit in the morning, you need to select a top, bottom, and shoes. You start out with the item of clothing you really want to wear, and you pick the most logical choices of what will go with it. Sometimes you wish you could wear a pair of pants with that perfect top, only to discover they are in the laundry, or you know the pants you want, find the perfect shirt, but notice there is a big spot on the front of the shirt. If you can manage through that part of your day, you can certainly make adaptations in the kitchen. Frequently I think of the perfect side dish to go with my protein, but then realize I'm missing a key ingredient in the recipe, and have to adjust accordingly.

To avoid that problem, start with knowing your inventory. Pantries, refrigerators, and freezers packed with junk and leftovers that need to be tossed make it difficult to know what you actually have on hand. Clean out the fridge and toss condiments that were opened years ago. All of the items that can be stored in a pantry should be categorized with jar, cans, and boxes, or choose the system that lets you know what you have at a moment's glance.

With fresh vegetables, start by using the vegetable that will go bad first. If it's something simple like lettuce, then it's like wearing a white shirt… anything goes with it. If it's something more exotic, like eggplant, your options for a meat or bean dish become more limited. I always choose the simple carbohydrate last and typically, it's a potato or a variety of rice. It can also be a tortilla, bread, or corn, (which I consider more of a grain than a vegetable) or another healthful grain like quinoa. I call these combinations of proteins, vegetables, and carbs "Triangle Meals" and with kids, the Triangle Meal concept helps them identify proper choices and quantify proper portions.

When I begin with a picky eater, I start with a huge portion of what they do like followed by a smaller portion of something that's just "okay," followed with one food that may not be their favorite, and is limited to just one bite. As an example, many children love French fries, so you start with a handful of fries, a smaller serving of hamburger, and one slice of cucumber. Within a short period, depending on your starting point, you can move the quantities of the slice of cucumber to three bites, and even out the hamburger portion to match the French fry portion. The "Three Bite Rule" may be in place for a year or so. They don't have to eat a whole serving, but they do have to eat three bites. When the rule never changes, kids know what is expected. After that has been a rule for a while (and only you know how much time to give it), you can start making equal portions the meal standard.

Disclaimer: I must say that I created some really bad food experiments in my life, and even I didn't want to eat three bites of some of the more memorable foods. There is no reason to force down inedible food, but if you've tasted it, and it's not that bad—even if they really don't "like it," they can swallow it down with a glass of water and chase it with something they do like.

Now you may be questioning if every meal needs to be a "Triangle" of threes. I get asked all the time, "What about pizza?" Pizza can either be loaded with vegetables and meat, or it can simply be a side dish for a meal that provides a protein and a vegetable. If you do a meat-based pizza, then serve a salad with it.

There are lots of ways to create the healthy "Triangle" approach to meals. There are some recipes where everything is "all in one." Many healthy casseroles, pasta dishes, and soups provide all three. I tell my clients to toss a stew or soup together in the Crock-pot before leaving for work in the morning so they can come home to a hot and healthy meal.

Healthy Snacks

Yes, it's possible to use the words "healthy" and "snacks" in the same sentence! With a little pre-planning, there's no reason why you can't have snacks ready in the refrigerator, packed in a lunch box, or tossed into the diaper bag or purse for nutritious and delicious pick-me-ups for hungry tummies. Here are some favorites for kids of all ages:

- Cut up raw vegetables
- Cut up raw fruits
- Frozen fruit
- Bean dips
- Guacamole
- Fresh salsa
- Yogurt dips and smoothies (Made with organic plain yogurt and sweetened with fresh fruit or raw honey as age appropriate.)
- Whole grain tortillas for dipping
- Whole grain breads with nut butters
- Muffins packed with vegetables or dried fruit and nuts
- Hard-boiled eggs
- Organic Jerky
- Toasted nuts and seeds
- Homemade oatmeal cookies loaded with nuts and raisins

Whatever Works—Eating Outside the Box

When Joey was little, he loved food that just about anyone would have deemed unusual. Sandwiches made with two pancakes, beans with coconut milk, and fried bologna were some of his favorites. Since my goal was to get him to eat a healthy diet, I was more than happy to create meals for him based on what he liked, and happily tossed my ideas of conventional and "normal" food combinations out the window.

Fast forward to 2009. While in Austria, I kept seeing the same menu item, "Fritatten Suppe," at a number of local restaurants. The translation for it was "clear broth with strips of pancakes."

"Surely it must be a translation error," I said to my husband as we ate one delicious meal after another. Finally my curiosity got the better of me, and I ordered the "mystery soup." When it came to the table, there was no mystery. It was just that: a clear broth with strips of pancakes put in the bowl. Joey would have loved it.

I speak a lot about getting your children to eat a large variety of foods, but that doesn't mean you need to ignore their cravings altogether. If your children want what you would consider to be a strange combination, as long as it seems to be a healthy choice, let them go with it. Who knows, it may become a national dish someday!

When the Parent is Picky

I frequently am introduced to parents who are such extreme picky eaters themselves that they are more fearful that they will have to change than their child. They don't expect their child to eat anything that they wouldn't eat themselves, so they assume their child won't eat foods that they personally dislike. I remember hearing one mom in a grocery store:

Child: "Mommy, can I have some of those crackers?"

Mom: "You won't like them, they have nuts."

The child paused and was really thinking.

Child: "Why don't I like nuts, again?"

Mom: "Because they are icky."

You may not be this extreme with your children, but they will model your behavior. They want to drink and eat what is familiar to them, and their first exposure to foods is in your home. Children who get a wide variety of foods when they are young are far more likely to remain good eaters throughout their lifetime.

Try to take a hard look at the potential cause of your picky eating:

Do you have addictions to Excitotoxins, gluten, dairy, or high fructose corn syrup?

Were you raised on a poor diet and never had exposure to a wide variety of foods?

Are you addicted to carbs because they are convenient, and you don't want to cook?

Do you have texture sensitivities?

Do you have negative memories of being forced to eat food you hated as a child?

Was mealtime a negative experience in your household?

Did you eat meals together as a family?

The last point is more powerful than you may think. From my experience, I believe that families that share meals together are less likely to produce picky eaters. The child that is left to feed himself or is prepared a special meal that is eaten alone is not exposed to the model of a varied diet. However, sitting down to dinner does not always mean a positive experience. Yelling or badgering your child at the dinner table will eventually create a negative connotation around food. Maybe this was the case in your own family. As you raise your children, look to the dinner table as a place of love. You may say, "It doesn't seem very loving if I have to make sure they eat their vegetables," but you do not need to make your request in a condescending way. Here are examples of a discussion you may have:

"I'm so glad we went over the new rules about three bites BEFORE we sat down at the table. I really enjoy our meals together, and now that you know what is expected, we can talk about fun things tonight."

If the child is starting an argument or refusing to follow the new rules, try, "I am not going to force you to eat dinner, but I want you to know that the menu will not change all night and the food doesn't taste as good once it's cold. If you get hungry in an hour, there are no other choices other than what I made to eat."

You MUST mean this. If two hours later out of fear of sending your child to bed hungry, you make him a sandwich, you have simply and powerfully taught him that if he waits long enough, you will give him what he asked for hours ago.

For the younger or non verbal child, you may find Triangle meals work best by allowing them to feed themselves the bite of food they want and putting the food YOU want them to eat on their fork between bites. This worked great with Joey. He still had the independence to eat from his plate, but even without verbal skills, he understood that if we put the piece of meat on the fork, he should take that bite next.

What If the Food I Cook Doesn't Taste Good?

When I wrote this book, I was afraid that a well-meaning parent (who also happened to be the worst cook imaginable), would create disgusting culinary creations masked as "healthy food," and their picky eater would write me a decade later, blaming me for their gastronomical torture as a child. Some food is just plain awful.

I have my own food "horror story"—the day I made fish fry for Joey. As the fish was still frying, I would take the cooked pieces over to Joey, insisting that he eat them. I hovered over him as he slowly swallowed each bite with a disgusted look on his little face. When John and I sat down to eat our dinner, I realized the fish was bad. Actually, it was terrible. It tasted just like ammonia, and was not even edible for the cat. Poor Joey. He was such a brave soldier, dutifully eating that awful food. After a lot of crying, (from me, not Joey), I declared from that day on, I would never serve anything without trying it first. I have since learned that using fresh food in its whole form is the best way to avoid a recipe disaster.

It's too bad that real cooking is rarely taught anymore, either at home, or in school. Home economic classes teach kids how to make sugary sweets instead of the basics we should all know, like meatloaf, pot roast, homemade chicken stock, and salad dressing. The Internet and the Food Network channel are filling some of the educational void. Both men and women can learn the fundamentals of food shopping and preparation. Cooking is a team sport! If one person hates to cook, there's always clean-up duty. Turning it into a family event makes cooking a time to connect and have fun. Everyone benefits from home cooked meals. Even better, it's far less expensive than eating out or take-out food.

Just because a recipe doesn't turn out the way you expected, and it's not everyone's instant favorite doesn't mean you have to throw it away. Sometimes an, "I guess it's okay." is an acceptable substitute for "Wow! This is delicious!" I am still reminded in my home about my sunflower seed burgers. The kids recognized my die-hard enthusiasm for them, so they compensated by eating as little as they could get away with. Those sunflower seed burgers became the babysitter's favorite threat:

"If you don't behave and clean your room, your mom said you were going to get sunflower seed burgers for dinner!"

I was told that the threat always worked, and for the record, once I found out how they really felt about the burgers, I never made them again.

Your Creative Kitchen

Whether or not you practice Feng Shui, most cooks agree that their kitchen has a certain feel to it that either supports flow or creates blocks. There are those who view their kitchen as Grand Central Station where chaos is what creates the beat and rhythm in their preparation. For others, the kitchen may work like an operating room with an overabundance of organization and perfection. I find pleasure from cooking in a loosely choreographed dance that moves with fluidity. Regardless of your personal cooking style, there are three components of your kitchen that can contribute to your desire to cook: Organization, Tools, and Creativity.

Organization – This is NOT Your Mother's Kitchen

It's easy to judge oneself when it comes to organization. I frequently have my picky eating clients tell me they are not organized cooks, and the word "organization" literally creates panic. What I notice, though, is that their standard of organization stems from comparing themselves to others. They visit neighbors whose homes are spotless, or recall their mother's tiny kitchen where she was able to produce massive meals. It's time to create your own form of organization: One that coordinates with your lifestyle, and especially your family's. Here are a few tips that have worked for me:

Kitchen counters, open and inviting, tend to be the drop off point for homework, mail, or the junk d' jour. Find a closed spot or other room for those bills and countless pieces of paper. Keep a calendar to help remind you of appointments instead of notes all over the refrigerator. If you must have a TV in your kitchen, I suggest you only watch shows that make you happy. Food Network is great, or anything that makes you laugh is good kitchen fare. I personally do not have a TV in the kitchen, as cooking is my meditation time, so music is a better accompaniment. Put away condiments that clutter counters. Store fruits that shouldn't be refrigerated, such as tomatoes, in nice bowls or hanging baskets. Make healthy snacks readily available. When you buy a bag of apples, put a few out and refrigerate the rest.

How often do you really use that hot dog bun warmer? Then why is it sitting on your counter? Across America, kitchen counters are flooded with appliances that people use once a month or less. I have a shelf at the bottom of my basement stairs for kitchen appliances and cookware that I don't use weekly. (Before I had a basement, I used my garage.) I hang my wok from a hook on the wall and coffee/tea mugs on hooks under a counter. I don't own a microwave. I keep only three appliances out: My toaster oven, my Kitchen Aid mixer, and my Vita-mix blender. I also keep my knives accessible and sharp. I have an open shelf above my stove for frequently used spices and cooking oils, and an open shelf for serving bowls.

In many kitchens I have visited, I am baffled at the impracticality in kitchen cabinet contents. I have seen entire cabinets in small kitchens filled with China and crystal that are only used once per year. The cabinets closest to your dishwasher save time when they house your everyday plates, glasses, and eating utensils. Don't clutter cabinets with every piece of cookware you own. How many stove burners do you have? Four? Then you may only need four pots. Choose the best variety of sizes and pack the others away. The same thing goes with baking. Do you use the Easter Bunny cake mold all year round? If not, pack it away with Easter decorations. Do you own Dora the Explorer plastic glasses that your daughter wouldn't be caught dead with now? Say good-bye and deal with the fact she's growing up. If you have another child down the road, she probably isn't going to care about Dora anyway. There is nothing wrong with plastic character glasses, but when everyone is avoiding them in the cupboard, they are taking up precious space.

Group your non-perishable items in the cupboard or pantry. Did you ever wonder why you ended up with four jars of mustard? It's probably because you didn't know you already had three jars. A system will help you locate ingredients faster, whether items are grouped by size, category, or storage type, whether it's cans, glass jars, or boxes. Keep all your baking ingredients in one place to make baking more enjoyable. Go through your spices. When my mother passed away, we found spices that were 40 years old. Spices lose their flavor—if you have any ground spices older than five years (and I'm pushing it here), throw them away. If the spice is in whole form, it will last much longer. Keep spices in airtight glass jars and away from the heat and light. I keep some of my favorite spices by the stove, but I use them so frequently, they don't have time to go bad!

Being on a budget doesn't have to mean you have to look at ugly plates every day. Between eBay, second hand stores, garage sales, and clearance department stores, you can find great deals on wild and fun plates. So what if they eventually chip? It adds character. I love my bright red (a color that stimulates the appetite) plates, but if I tire of the color in a couple of years, then I'll choose another. I do, however, like things to match in my kitchen, but going through themes can be fun. For years, I settled on neutral décor and plates because I felt it was more practical. Now that I'm older, I enjoy the fun of a bright and colorful kitchen. For you, beige may feel comforting and clean. There is not a right or wrong. Go with what makes you happy.

Keep your fridge "ick" free. Throw away that five year-old chutney that you will never touch. Keep vegetables in special bags that prolong their life and tuck them in produce drawers that control humidity. I have a morning habit of cleaning out what I know will not get eaten. I get rid of herbs, vegetables, and fruits that are starting to wilt by making breakfast smoothies, homemade chicken stock, and meatloaf with pureed vegetables.

Buy a fun apron and stop telling people you don't cook. You can cook, you have just chosen not to up until now, and that story can change. Stop using the excuse that you are a horrible cook to get out of cooking. We ALL are horrible cooks at one period of our lives, but for those of us who now enjoy cooking, we made enough mistakes that we finally figured out how to use those errors to our advantage. The first time I made lasagna, I didn't know you had to boil the noodles first. It was humiliating, as I was serving it at a dinner party! Get out of your comfort zone, make some mistakes, and play with your food! It also helps to take a few cooking classes. We are so blessed to live in a time when cooking classes and shows on television and the Internet are widely available.

Kitchen Essentials – Tools of the Trade

Carpenters, doctors, and artists—every craftsman needs the proper tools to do their work. Cooking is no different. Having the right implements close at hand makes meal creation much easier and more enjoyable. How many times have you tried pounding a nail with a screwdriver? Take the time to invest in a few quality kitchen tools, and you'll thank yourself every day when you reach into the drawer and pull out your favorite knife. And speaking of knives:

Knives

For preparing fresh food, there is nothing more valuable in the kitchen than a really good knife. You don't need a huge set. Although other knives do have their purpose, for food preparation you can get by with a quality chef knife, a paring knife, and a serrated knife. I would rather have you own three great knives than 20 bad ones. And please, don't forget to sharpen your knife each time you use it. I wash mine, sharpen it, and then put it away. It takes just seconds, and it will speed up your prep time, and make it more enjoyable when you can always reach for a sharp and fast cutting knife.

Cutting Board

Along with a good knife, you need a good chopping block. Bamboo boards are my favorite. I suggest a tiny one for herbs, garlic, cheese, and small items; a large one for serious vegetable cutting, and because of the bacteria, and another large one just for cutting meat. The one for meat is curved up so the juice doesn't run off the sides.

Blender

Although a strong blender is fine, I really love the versatility of the Vita-mix blender. It juices, grinds grains, and my favorite feature is its ability to handle hot liquids. A good blender can also do the job, but sharpen your blade regularly or buy a new blade every few years for best performance.

Food Processor

A good food processor is also handy and I like to have two different sizes. I use a large one for chopping and grating, and have a very small one that blends salad dressings, chops herbs and garlic, as well as nuts. Coffee grinders also work well for nuts.

Stoneware

I love stoneware for all of my baking. Aluminum pans will seep aluminum into your food, and aluminum and other heavy metals are believed to be a contributing factor of Alzheimer's and Autism Spectrum Disorders.

Cast Iron

I have a few stainless steel pots, but prefer to cook in cast iron whenever possible as a frequently used cast iron pan is naturally non-stick. Non-stick surfaces can be made of dangerous chemicals and the ease of cast iron is often overlooked for expensive cookware. When cooking with cast iron, it's important to always heat the pan first, and then add your oil, and then the food. Affordable cast iron is usually available at hardware stores, sporting good stores, and discount centers. Cast iron cookware should only be rinsed, dried, and oiled; there's no need to soap and scrub the pans after each use.

Wok

There are few cookware items as versatile as the wok. It's also a great tool when teaching your children to cook, because the ingredients don't spill out as easily, and they get a wide view. I bought my steel wok at an Asian store and it was very affordable. I don't remember what color it used to be, because it's turned very dark from years of use.

No Microwaves

I know they are a kitchen staple, but I don't like microwaves. They destroy the nutrition of your food by cooking from the inside out, breaking open the foods' natural cellular fluids. I like my DNA the way it is, and prefer not to have it altered by the microwave's electromagnetic waves while waiting for the butter to melt. It is not hard to take out a pot and warm up food. It tastes so much better than heating up leftovers in the microwave. Toaster ovens are great for single servings, and if anything else you make in the microwave doesn't fit into those parameters, maybe you shouldn't be eating it anyway. When was the last time you popped popcorn on the stove? It tastes like… popcorn!

Utensils

I have two drawers for utensils; one for frequently used, and one for occasionally used. I try to limit my impulse to buy every new gadget that comes on the market, as it just makes finding what you need in the crowded drawer more difficult, and many of the specialty items don't add that much in the way of convenience. A few of my favorites are good wooden spoons—especially the type that are flat for scraping the bottoms of pans. I like whisks in different sizes, as small ones are great for scrambled eggs and salad dressing. A lemon juicer is frequently overlooked, but I add lemon to many dishes and prefer not to have seeds. A meat thermometer is especially helpful to new cooks and even those of us who think we know when the chicken is done. Stainless steel flipper spatulas work so much better as long as you are not working on non-stick coated surfaces. Spatulas for scraping the bowl are better with a good flexible material.

Bowls

I admit that I'm all about the bowl. Maybe it's my Italian heritage, but I love the feeling of serving pasta in painted bowls or salads in sturdy wooden bowls. I like colorful vegetables in thick white bowls and fruit salads in clear glass. Will this make your child eat more vegetables? I have no idea, I just feel better when the food is presented well, and I'm sure that somehow that energy has to pass its way into my food. Interestingly, when I teach picky eating strategies for many of my families, I control portions by preparing their plate myself so serving bowls are not as necessary. Eventually, every meal is more democratic served family style. When the picky eater knows what is expected of them, they might enjoy the food presentation. When I cook, I use large stainless steel bowls. Don't be afraid to use a larger bowl than you think you may need. I see cooks unsuccessfully trying to keep all the ingredients in a small bowl while they are stirring, when the use of a larger bowl adds possibly five seconds more to clean up time and makes it so much easier to prepare the food properly!

Character-Ware

This is my pet term for plates, cups, and bowls with pictures of the Disney character or kid celebrity of the month. It's usually made from cheap plastic that is completely indestructible, BUT it can be a huge tool in associating what kids love with food. The other nice quality of character-ware is that the plates are often divided into triangle sections, making it easy to serve protein, vegetables, and simple carbs.

Kitchen Essentials—Stocking the Pantry

This list may not be complete, or reflect your kitchen, because of the fact that we all enjoy different types of food. I am mostly Italian, but have a tremendous love of Eastern cuisine, especially Thai and Indian. What I can "never" be without is not what you may feel is necessary at all. However, because this book is focused on getting your picky eater to eat healthy foods, I will focus on highlighting cookware and healthy staples that I use in my own home.

Appliances	Bake Ware	Utensils	Cookware
Blender or Vita Mix Bread maker Crock-pot Gas or Electric grill Juicer Kitchen Aid mixer Rice cooker Toaster oven Tortilla maker	Casserole dishes in the sizes that fit your family Cupcake pans (mini & large) Non-Aluminum Cookie sheets/ Bar pans Loaf pans (mini & large) Pie pans	Bread knife Chef knife Paring knife Steak knives Knife sharpener Bamboo or wood spoons and flat spoons Bulb baster Masher Pizza cutter Spatulas (for flipping and scrapping) Strainer for skimming Whisk (mini & large) Tongs Zester/Grater	Cast iron frying pan Ceramic casserole pot (capable of stove top and oven) Stackable stainless steel bowls Stainless steel or other non-aluminum quality pots 4-6 multiple sizes Wok

Misc. Tools	Spices	Herbs	Baking Ingredients
Lemon juicer	Allspice	Basil	Baking powder
Meat thermometer	Bay leaf	Bouquet Garni	Baking soda
Cutting boards (wood or bamboo – large & mini)	Cardamom (whole)	Dill	Cocoa powder/ Carob powder
Colander	Chili powder	Garlic	Tapioca
Garni bags-used for holding fresh herbs in soups and stews	Chilies	Herbs de Provence	Vanilla
	Cinnamon	Marjoram	Yeast
	Clove	Oregano	
	Coriander (ground)	Parsley	
	Cumin	Rosemary	
	Curry (Sweet)	Sage	
	Garam Masala	Tarragon	
	Ginger	Thyme	
	Mustard-dry		
	Nutmeg		
	Paprika		
	Pepper		
	Sea salt		
	Seasoned salt		
	Tandoori Masala		
	Turmeric		

Sweeteners	**Regular Flours & Grains**	**Gluten-Free Flours** (If on a gluten-free diet)	**Oils and Fats** (All cold & expeller pressed, preferably organic)
Brown sugar Maple syrup (Grade B has more nutrition) Molasses Powdered sugar Raw local honey Unbleached cane sugar	Corn meal Oats (whole) Spelt White wheat Whole wheat	Amaranth Arrowroot Bean flours Buckwheat Corn Millet Montina Nut flours Oats (certified Gluten-free) Pea flour Potato flour and starch Quinoa Rice (all varieties) Sorghum Tapioca Teff	Avocado (high heat) Butter Coconut (excellent frying oil that withstands high temperatures) Ghee (Butter with the casein removed- popular in Eastern cuisine) Grape Seed Olive oil (for cooking, use standard extra virgin olive oil. Moderate heat only) Olive oil (high quality oil is a wonderful splurge for salad dressing, dipping, & coating cooked vegetables) Palm oil (high heat) Sun/Safflower oil Walnut oil (wonderful for salads, no heat)

Pantry Items and Condiments	Canned Goods	Beans	Raw Nut and Seed Staples
Apple cider Capers Coconut milk Fish sauce Hoisin sauce Hot sauce Ketchup Mayonnaise Mirin sauce Mustard-different varieties Olives Oyster sauce Pickles Steak sauce Tamari or soy sauce Vinegars (Low acid such as Raspberry, Balsamic, & red wine) Worcestershire sauce	Peas Corn Green beans Pumpkin Tomato paste Tomato sauce Whole or diced tomatoes	Adzuki Baked beans Garbanzo Kidney Pinto Refried beans (black & pinto) White Northern	Almonds (slivered and blanched) Almond butter Hazelnuts Macadamia Peanut butter Pecans Sesame seeds Sunflower seeds Walnuts

Kitchen Essentials: Perishables

Meat, Poultry, & Fish

If you have the space at all, buy an extra freezer. The chest freezers are cheaper than the uprights. It can be in a basement, garage, or even a shed with electric power. Cost wise, it quickly adds up to a huge savings. Buying meats in bulk saves hundreds of dollars, and always having tonight's dinner just a quick defrost away will save you money on eating out and multiple grocery trips. Because I live by farms and have friends who are farmers, I buy 52 organic whole chickens once a year immediately after processing. They stay in their own freezer in a deep freeze and once a week I pull one out for meals, and making stock or soup. The farmer doesn't have to store them or sell them to a distributor. This isn't a choice for everyone, but even if you just have a close relationship with your local butcher, there are great deals for bulk if you purchase the meat right after processing so that they don't have to store it.

Bulk Groceries

Buying clubs are shifting our purchases into bulk, but these stores are still very limited in their stocking of healthy options. Health food stores are generally happy to sell to you in bulk for a 5-10% discount if you ask. Like the meat, the issue for them is storage and shelf space, so if you commit to a case, they pass the savings right over to you. Also, you can request items they don't normally carry. Many items are available from their distributor, but if they only have a limited amount of shelf space, you many never see it in their store. However, remember that natural groceries may have a shorter shelf life, and if your family grows tired of the item, and you only go through half of the case before it expires, then you lose money.

Eating Out

Dining in America

John and I were grabbing a quick bite of wonderful Italian food at a local restaurant in a touristy area of Wisconsin on a rainy summer evening. As my eye was on the door, I watched a man run out of his minivan and dash inside with his burning question, "Do you have a children's menu?" You could see the hopefulness in his eyes. It was early in the evening on a Sunday, and there would be no waiting at any restaurant, but I could read in that dad's face, "I just want dinner in an adult restaurant." The hostess said, "We don't have a kid's menu, but we are happy to adapt anything we have."

"Fair enough," the dad answered, and ran to get his family.

In walked a very angry-looking mom and two young children about four and six years old. They sat down at their table with its lovely white tablecloth and napkins, and were served water with lemon and fresh Italian bread right out of the oven. The children were behaving nicely. As they all sat down, the mom shot her husband an, "I can't believe you dragged us in here" look.

"There is nothing here that the kids will eat," hissed the mom across the table to the hungry dad.

Now let me just say that even the pickiest of eaters I know will typically eat a bowl of pasta with butter or a meatball. Perhaps it was chicken nuggets, burgers, or French fries they were looking for, but the kids were not going to get those choices in the exact preformed American way. The mom abruptly stood up, and the little boy said, "Mommy, why are we leaving?"

The mom snapped, "They have nothing for you to eat. Let's go."

Dad apologized to the hostess, and out they fled to the fast food restaurant next door. It broke my heart and made me angry all at the same time. Do parents like that even recognize that they have choices?

The reality of family life today is often a schedule that barely allows enough time to open a can of soup. I definitely believe in the need for the "family dinner table," but I also understand that some families have lifestyles that leave few options for a communal evening meal. Whether you are the single parent with a long commute that barely makes it home before the kids need to be in bed, or the parent of children in every possible sport and activity invented by the park district, meals may not be a priority, yet you are probably well aware that most fast food allows little in terms of nutrition. And let's face it, there is rarely any complaining when you go pull up to the drive through window and customize everyone's request.

There are a large number of parents who simply don't like to cook. I can't criticize this—I don't like to clean, so I have help for that. More power to you if you're lucky enough to live in a city that gives you lots of food choices, and your budget allows you to eat out frequently and well.

In all cases, you do have menu options. There is a dramatic difference, however, if you live in Whitewater, Wisconsin vs. San Francisco, California. You could live in San Francisco and go to a different restaurant every night for a year, and get amazingly tasty, economic, and healthy options. However, if you live in an isolated rural area, your choices may be decent, bad, and horrible. (Hence the reason I learned how to cook!)

Healthy Tips for Eating Out

1. Don't even ask for the "Kids' Menu."

Kids' restaurant menus contain some of the least nutritious foods on the planet—complete with silly names, and limited healthy choices. What is that? Think about it. Why would we accept and support this purely American bad habit of saving the worst foods for the growing bodies and minds of our children?

2. Order appetizers.

This is a great way to try small amounts of new foods. Instead of a large meal, order two appetizers. Crab cakes, chicken wings, and guacamole are all gentle and likeable foods that appeal to most appetites.

3. Split meals.

My kids are teenagers, but we still do this because we like to try more than one choice. Another great option is to order appetizers and split a meal. Size wise this equals out the same as an entrée and kids meal, but you are more likely to see some form of a vegetable this way.

4. Order vegetables on the side.

When ordering in a restaurant, an even better option is to split the meal, and order extra vegetables on the side. This works out well whether you are ordering a hamburger and fries or a steak and baked potato. Most restaurants have a vegetable of the day, or you can try the salad menu for wonderful raw choices.

5. Go ethnic.

(By ethnic, I don't mean Taco Bell.) Typically, ethnic food has a greater potential for vegetables than American food. Here are some examples of foods to look for:

Mexican – A great time to eat beans! Try guacamole, fresh salsa, and fajitas (with grilled vegetables and meat or fish).

Chinese – So they love Sweet and Sour Chicken? Okay, but order some type of vegetable stir-fry to accompany it. If they love fried rice, mix the veggie stir-fry into the fried rice.

Thai – It's almost impossible not to eat healthy with Thai food. Go for foods rich in coconut (wonderful fat). Chicken Satay is pleasing to most picky eaters, and cucumber salad is one of the easiest vegetables to push.

Indian – Once again, it's almost all good. Picky eaters will love Naan, but have them at least dip it in a curry or chutney sauce. Even if they don't eat the curry at first, the spices are some of the highest antioxidants foods you can eat.

Middle Eastern – Kabobs are fun for kids because they are on a stick and separate. Picky eaters usually have a problem with combined foods and kabobs are individual pieces. You can also get great nutrition from dips, such as hummus, for both pitas and fresh veggies.

Japanese – Start with Edamame (fun little boiled soy beans that are easier to digest than most versions of soy) and tempura. Tempura may not be the healthiest choice, but as long as they eat more than the outside breading, it's a good acclimation to vegetables and shrimp.

A Global Perspective

My lifelong passion for food is equally matched by an enthusiastic love of traveling. Travel has always been a priority for me, and over the years I have explored and enjoyed a variety of cultures on all sides of the globe. No matter where in the world I went, I studied the eating habits of children.

In Thailand, I watched in amazement as toddlers ate meats with chili peppers so hot they would have sent most Americans screaming for water. I have been to poor villages where the children enjoyed healthier food that wealthy American children would ever willingly pass through their lips. I have been told by a ten year old in Hungary how to make goulash, been amazed by Italian teenagers that preferred water to soft drinks, and watched high school kids in Austria purposely order vegetables without their parents looking over their shoulders.

In a discussion with a friend of mine who has toddlers and lives in Budapest, I asked him about picky eating. He had never heard of the term, even though his English was perfect. I asked him what children typically ate in Budapest. He took me to a few restaurants where we searched for a "Children's Menu." Even in the family friendly diner, we could not find one. He told me that traditional Hungarian food (They are known for their many wonderful soups) was still cheaper than McDonalds.

I was disappointed, but not surprised, to find children's menus in the Americanized hotels in Budapest. Appealing to tourists, they offered the standardized chicken strips, macaroni and cheese, pizza, and probably hot dogs. Apparently America's bad eating habits are creeping across the globe.

Don't get me wrong—there are growing numbers of enthusiastic and healthy eaters in the United States these days, but we're a long way from the norm. Fast food still has a choke hold on the hearts and wallets of too many Americans, and processed convenience foods still grace far too many dinner tables.

I can only hope that other countries hold on to their traditional roots of real food. The recent infusion of new cuisines, ingredients, and food options into our country is a welcome shift. There is tremendous pleasure to be had in appreciating ingredients that have been hand picked, slow cooked, and brought to us from a recipe that has lasted for centuries. I love and respect regional food and its heritage, and I have heartfelt appreciation for homes and restaurants, wherever they are, that serve real food with pride, and most importantly, love.

Special Occasions

What is Christmas without cookies and rich desserts? For birthdays, of course you need cake. Halloween and candy go together like witches and brooms. Office parties, neighborhood get-togethers, snacks and sports on TV, pre-school treats… pretty soon every day is a special food occasion with caution and good nutrition thrown to the wind.

Food should be special—even today, I wouldn't give up those "hot chocolate and cookies" Christmas mornings when we were so excited to open presents that we skipped cooking breakfast. But it's so easy to fall into the never-ending trap of "special occasions." When my children were little, I would allow candy on Halloween Day for the girls. But then they would take all but a few favorites, and put the rest in a bag on the front porch. The "Great Pumpkin" would scoop up the candy at night and leave them a toy. Amazingly, at 16 and 13, they still expect me to do that! One day of high-fructose corn syrup indulgence is usually okay for some children, but really think about how often you want to do that to their growing bodies. If you don't set clear guidelines, it becomes a constant negotiation. How many of us recognize this:

"But Mom, all the other kids are eating candy… drinking soda… having snacks… choosing sugar-filled donuts." Where do you draw the line?

Here are some tips to avoid "special occasion" overload:

Lay down the rules before the party or event. "This is how many treats you are allowed." or "You can have cake, BUT first you have to eat five vegetables from the veggie tray and at least half of a hamburger."

If you don't know if something nutritious will be served, bring it or eat before you go. Having a birthday party at Chuck E. Cheese or McDonalds? Then say, "Before you leave, please eat this natural peanut butter on a celery stick."

When your children are toddlers, be sure and let relatives and close friends know that you have chosen not to introduce processed or sweet foods into your child's diet, but be gentle, as it's a natural impulse to feed children sweets and treats. I once gave my sugar-free one-year old nephew Ronan a lick of my ice cream. I knew better, but wasn't even thinking that if he had it once, he'd be hooked on the taste. My wonderful niece, Carrie laughingly said, "Aunt Betsy, you of all people should know better." He was just so cute that I totally lost sight of the situation and her wishes. Gently remind Grandma, who loves your child so much, that little ones have different taste buds, and she doesn't need to use all of that sugar in a cookie to please your toddler.

School snacks are one of the biggest pet peeves of many parents who work very hard preparing healthy meals at home. It becomes peer pressure for the child, and a frustrating situation for the parent trying to maintain a healthy diet for their child. It used to really bother me when my kids were little and their teachers used candy as rewards. How can you blame a second grader for eating the gummy bears when told that they earned them for doing well, and everyone else is gobbling them down? Because my children were gluten and casein-free as grade schoolers, I used to send in my own treats; usually cupcakes or dairy free ice cream cups that they could keep in the freezer and take out for someone's birthday or for earning a reward.

My youngest daughter, Jessie, was really sensitive about being "different," and other kids acted like something was wrong with her when she brought treats from home. Even though there are so many non-allergenic treats that are healthy and that most kids would like, the few that were picky eaters would criticize the unfamiliar treat, reducing my daughter to tears. I would like to see policies in school that promote only healthy food choices in the classrooms. If your child has special needs, the best you can do at this time is to discuss the situation with the teacher so that your child is comfortable with her treat.

Putting It All Together

So now you sit almost finished with the book and images of cooperative family meals are starting to float in. You actually feel like this is all possible, but where do you begin? Here is a step-by-step guide to implementing the techniques and ideas I have included throughout the book:

1. Visualize what it is you want and write it down.

Sometimes I will speak to parents who have come so far and never stop to pat themselves on the back. I say to them, "Look how far you have come!" and they say, "Yes, but we have so far to go." It is hard to feel a sense of accomplishment when you expect more from yourself and your child than either one of you is able to achieve all at once. Here is a sample of a patient's list:

Month One: Michael will eat three bites of meat once a day.

Month Two: Michael will additionally eat three bites of vegetables once a day.

Month Three: Michael will eat three bites of meat twice per day.

And so on. Both you and your child need to celebrate the progress and not fret if you had a difficult month. If you have a month where you experienced nutritional set backs, please don't give up. Try to pick up where you left off, or backtrack a little if need be. One month is a very short period of time in a child's life. As difficult as progress seems, I would much rather have you take it slower than give up completely.

2. Talk to the children or make picture books.

If they are developed enough to understand language, go over your goals with them. See if they have any of their own. Involve them in all of the processes and decisions that you can. The more they understand, the more cooperative they will be. If your child has limited verbal communication, make them a picture book that helps them to understand the process of what you are doing.

3. Clean out the kitchen.

The day I found out how bad high fructose corn syrup was, I reached a tipping point and put my anger into the cupboard where I threw out cereal boxes, spaghetti sauce, cookies, candy, soda, and anything else that had high fructose corn syrup, MSG, and artificial coloring, sweetening, and flavoring. As I learned more, I also threw away my aluminum pots and pans, rearranged cabinets, and cleaned my refrigerator and freezer in preparation of the organic whole food that would be entering my home.

4. Go grocery shopping.

Start by checking out your grocery choices and figure out what items you want to buy and where. Maybe a local butcher will become your new friend as he helps you select tonight's dinner. You may do you bulk shopping at one store, and your specialty foods at another. Ask people, whose diet you respect, where they shop. Become friends with your local health food storeowner. Ask about saving on bulk items. If you don't have a good local source for organic foods, then plan to shop at least once a month at the store closest to you. To stock up, I will drive one hour to Madison, Wisconsin to do major grocery shopping.

5. Plan your meals.

You now know what to eat and where to buy it. Organize these ideas with a meal planner. You can purchase these, download them, or simply take a blank piece of paper, and make seven columns and four rows. Each column represents a day of the week, each row, Breakfast, Lunch, Dinner, Snacks. For those on restrictive diets, you can have an immune benefit from rotating foods, but for most of you, simply spread out the types of foods as best you can to add variety. After years of meal planning, I now only meal plan my dinners. Breakfasts are more self-serve, and lunches are last night's dinner leftovers.

6. Begin doing the techniques.

The chapter on sensory integration strategies allows you to customize where to begin; I usually recommend waiting until the previous steps are done before you dive into the actual techniques. Get the kitchen, yourself, and your child ready and feel settled into your decision. If you choose a technique that is too advanced, just step back a level, but don't stop.

Conclusion

Last week I made a wonderful vegetable soup and my youngest daughter wouldn't touch it. I said, "C'mon Jess, just three bites." She rolled her eyes at me and left the room as if to say, "Mom, give it up." My first thought was, "What will people say when I am a published author on picky eating, and my daughter is sitting in the school cafeteria munching on nacho chips with fake cheese sauce?"

I'm hoping they'll say that everyone eventually makes their own choices. We are all free to make our own choices. When our children are small, we have a great power of influence, but as they get older, and as it should be, they get to make their own decisions. What I have learned from my journey is that all we can truly accomplish is to plant the seeds of sound nutrition and positive choices, and hope that those seeds bear the fruit of joyful and healthy eating for a lifetime.

Buon Appetito!

References

1. Severson, Kim. "Picky Eaters? They Get It From You." New York Times. October 10, 2007. http://www.nytimes.com/2007/10/10/dining/10pick.html (accessed September 2009)

2. National Cancer Institute. Cancer SEER Stat Fact Sheets. Stats 2009. http://seer.cancer.gov/statfacts/html/all.html (accessed January 2010)

3. Balisunset. Hub Pages. "Fast Food and Soft Drink Marketing." http://hubpages.com/hub/Fast-Food-and-Soft-Drink-Marketing (accessed February 2010)

4. United States Department of Agriculture. Economic Research Service. Economic Information Bulletin No. EIB-19, October 2006. "Let's Eat Out: Americans Weigh Taste, Convenience, and Nutrition." http://www.ers.usda.gov/publications/eib19/ (accessed September 2009)

5. Smithers, Louis. "Omega 3 EPA DHA: Our Evolution in Food." Consumption Statistics, Associated Content. January 1, 2008. http://www.associatedcontent.com/article/323011/omega_3_epa_dha_our_evolution_in_food.html?cat=51/ (accessed October 2009)

6. United States Department of Agriculture. Economic Research Service. Publication No. 750. http://www.ers.usda.gov/publications/aib750/aib750i.pdf (accessed September 2009)

7. Edgar, Patricia. "Marketing to Children: a time-bomb." Young Media. http://www.youngmedia.org.au/pdf/marketing_children.pdf. (accessed October 2009)

8. United States Department of Agriculture. Economic Research Service. Publication 750. "America's Eating Habits Changes and Consequences." http://www.ers.usda.gov/publications/aib750/aib750i.pdf (accessed September 2009)

9. Colorado State University. "Physiology of Taste." http://www.vivo.colostate.edu/hbooks/pathphys/digestion/pregastric/taste.html (accessed January 2010)

10. Disabled-World. "Genetically Modified Food-GM Foods List and Information." http://www.disabled-world.com/fitness/gmfoods.php/(accessed January 2010)

11. Organic Consumers. "60-70% of ingredients in US are GMO." http://www.organicconsumers.org/articles/article_17979.cfm/ (accessed January 2010)

12. Agrability of Wisconsin. "Savor:Wisconsin Celebrates June Dairy Month." http://www.bse.wisc.edu/agrability/.219 (accessed December 2009)

13. American Celiac Disease Alliance. "Celiac Disease is 'In'." http://americanceliac.org/ (accessed February 2010)

14. Forristal, Linda Joyce. "The Murky World of High-Fructose Corn Syrup." Weston A Price. December 3, 2003. http://www.westonaprice.org/The-Murky-World-of-High-Fructose-Corn-Syrup.html/ (accessed December 2009)

15. Forristal, Linda Joyce. http://www.westonaprice.org/The-Murky-World-of-High-Fructose-Corn-Syrup.html/

16. Nancy Nelson. "The Majority of Cancers are Linked to the Environment." National Cancer Institute. Issue 3 Vol. 4, June 17, 2004. http://www.cancer.gov/newscenter/benchmarks-vol4issue3/page1 (accessed January 2010)

Glossary of Terms

Acid Reflux

Acid reflux, also known as heartburn, refers to a digestive condition in which gastric acid is regurgitated. Stomach acid rises up into the esophagus and throat and causes a painful burning sensation in the chest, throat, neck, and jaw.

Amino Acids

Amino acids are the chemical units or "building blocks" of the body that make up proteins. Protein substances make up the muscles, tendons, organs, glands, nails, and hair. Growth, repair, and maintenance of all cells are dependent upon them. Next to water, protein makes up the greatest portion of our body weight. Amino acids that must be obtained from the diet are called essential amino acids; other amino acids that the body can manufacture from other sources are called non-essential amino acids.

Anaerobic

Anaerobic means "not requiring oxygen." An anaerobic environment lacks oxygen. Anaerobic bacteria do not need oxygen to grow; in fact oxygen is toxic to them.

Anaphylactic Reactions

Also called anaphylaxis, an anaphylactic reaction is often triggered by allergen substances that are injected or ingested and thereby gain access into the bloodstream. An explosive reaction involving the skin, lungs, nose, throat, and gastrointestinal tract can then result. Although severe cases of anaphylaxis can occur within seconds or minutes of exposure and be fatal if untreated, many reactions are milder and can be ended with prompt medical therapy.

ATP

Adenosine triphosphate (ATP) is considered by biologists to be the energy currency of life. It is the high-energy molecule that stores the energy we need to do just about everything we do. It is present in the cytoplasm and nucleoplasm of every cell, and essentially all the physiological mechanisms that require energy for operation obtain it directly from the stored ATP. As food in the cells is gradually oxidized, the released energy is used to re-form the ATP so that the cell always maintains a supply of this essential molecule.

Autoimmune Disease

Autoimmune disease refers to an illness that occurs when the body tissues are attacked by the body's own immune system. The immune system is a complex organized network within the body that is designed to normally "seek and destroy" invaders of the body, including infectious agents. People with autoimmune disease frequently have atypical antibodies circulating in their blood that target their own body tissues. Common autoimmune diseases include arthritis, lupus, Celiac disease, diabetes, multiple sclerosis, Grave's disease, and Crohn's disease.

Bile

Bile is a yellow-green fluid that is made by the liver, stored in the gallbladder, and passes through the common bile duct into the duodenum (the first part of the small intestine) where it helps digest fat. The principle components of bile are cholesterol, bile salts, and the pigment bilirubin.

Biomedical

Biomedical is applied science dealing with health. There are two branches of biomedical research: the study and research of the food we eat and the study and research of health related issues to understand how humans and other animals function, as well as the application of knowledge to improve health and prevent and cure diseases.

Candida

Candida is a yeast-like parasitic fungus that can sometimes cause Thrush. Candida has the potential to cause disease, especially in people with low immunity. Candida overgrowth in the gut can cause various health problems like fatigue, weight gain, gastrointestinal distress, and "brain fog."

Carbohydrate

Carbohydrates are the main energy source for the human body. The basic building block of every carbohydrate is a sugar molecule, a simple union of carbon, hydrogen, and oxygen. Starches and fibers are essentially chains of sugar molecules. Some contain hundreds of sugars. The digestive system handles all carbohydrates in much the same way—it breaks them down (or tries to break them down) into single sugar molecules, since only these are small enough to cross into the bloodstream. It also converts most digestible carbohydrates into glucose (also known as blood sugar), because cells are designed to use this as a universal energy source.

There are two types of carbohydrates: simple and complex. Simple carbohydrates convert very quickly to blood sugar, often causing a rise in blood glucose levels. Sugar, fruit juices, fruit, and milk are examples of simple carbs. Complex carbohydrates are found in vegetables, beans, and whole grains. The nutrients and fiber in complex carbs slow the digestive process down, and the slow release of absorbable nutrients and sugar create a consistent level of energy and sugar levels. A new system, called the glycemic index, aims to classify carbohydrates based on how quickly and how high they boost blood sugar compared to pure glucose.

Casein

Casein is a protein that is found in milk and used independently in many foods as a binding agent. Technically, it is part of a group called phosphoproteins, collections of proteins bound to something containing phosphoric acid. Edible casein is widely used in both medicine and food, both for nutritional value and as a binder.

Celiac Disease

Celiac disease is an autoimmune disease, often inherited, in which the lining of the small intestine is damaged from eating gluten and other proteins found in wheat, barley, rye, and some oats. In a healthy intestinal tract, nutrients pass from the intestine into the bloodstream through the villi, tiny fingers that line the intestinal wall. The disease process damages and destroys the villi, preventing the body from getting sufficient nutrients from the food that is eaten. People with celiac disease must follow a gluten-free diet, as well as carefully watch for everyday products like medicines, vitamins, and even lip balm that may contain gluten.

Chyme

Chyme is pre-digested, acidified food mass that passes from the stomach into the small intestine in a semi-liquid state.

Cytokines

Cytokines are small, secreted proteins that mediate and regulate immunity and inflammation, and are involved in reproduction, growth and development, normal homeostatic regulation, and response to injury and repair, including blood clotting. They must be produced each time in response to an immune stimulus. They generally (although not always) act over short distances and short time spans and at very low concentration. They act by binding to specific membrane receptors, which then signal the cell via second messengers to alter its behavior.

DNA (Deoxyribonucleic acid)

DNA is a nucleic acid that contains the genetic instructions used in the development and functioning of all known living organisms and some viruses. The main role of DNA molecules is the long-term storage of information. DNA is often compared to a set of blueprints or a code, since it contains the instructions needed to construct other components of cells like proteins and RNA molecules. DNA segments that carry this genetic information are called genes, but other DNA sequences have structural purposes, or are involved in regulating the use of this genetic information.

Detoxification System

The detoxification system is the process of clearing toxins from the body, or neutralizing/transforming them from fat soluble to water-soluble so they can be excreted from the body, as well as clearing excess mucus and congestion. Many of these toxins come from our diet, drug use, and both chronic and acute environmental exposure. Inside the body, fats, especially oxidized fats, cholesterol, free radicals, and other irritating molecules also act as toxins. Poor digestion, colon sluggishness and dysfunction, reduced liver function, and poor elimination through the kidneys, respiratory tract, and skin all add to increased toxicity. There are two phases to the detoxification process and they are designed to work synergistically.

Phase I involves a group of enzymes called the Cytochrome 450 family. Phase I enzymes can neutralize some chemicals, but most toxins are converted to an intermediate form of the toxin, and in this intermediate stage are often more toxic than their original form, and require the action of Phase II to complete the de-tox cycle.

In Phase II, the liver adds a substance through a process called conjugation to neutralize the toxins and make them water-soluble, and therefore excretable through urine, sweat, stool, and hair. Phase II reactions may follow Phase I for some toxins, or act directly on the toxin in Phase II only. Glutathione plays an important role in Phase II detoxification. If one Phase is working more efficiently than the other, toxins may build up in the body, causing environmental allergies, hormonal imbalances, and may lead to chronic illness or some cancers.

Dopamine

Dopamine is a neurotransmitter that transmits signals between different neurons or nerve cells of the brain. Dopamine plays an important role in many functions of the brain, including human behavior, cognition, attention, movement, pleasure, hormonal processes, learning, and is especially associated with the response of the human brain to motivation and reward. Altered levels of dopamine in the brain can cause a range of problems and diseases such as Parkinson's, ADD, alcoholism, bi-polar disorder, schizophrenia, and depression.

Electrolytes

In chemistry, an electrolyte is any substance containing free ions that make the substance electrically conductive. In the body, electrolytes are minerals in the blood and other bodily fluids that carry an electric charge, such as sodium, potassium, and calcium. The level of electrolytes in the body, and their balance, affects the amount of water in the body, the acidity (pH) of the blood, and other important processes. Your body depends on electrolytes to help it perform vital functions and chemical reactions. Electrolytes are lost through perspiration, and replaced through drinking fluids.

Endorphins

Endorphins are an opiod (morphine-like) chemical produced by the body that serves as a natural painkiller to suppress pain. Endorphins are manufactured in the brain, spinal cord, as well as many other parts of the body. They are released in response to neurotransmitters and bind to certain neuron receptors—the same ones that bind opiate medicines. Endorphins act as analgesics, diminishing the perception of pain. They also act as sedatives, and can produce a euphoric opiod state.

Enzyme

An enzyme is a protein (or protein-based molecule) that speeds up a chemical reaction in a living organism. An enzyme acts as a catalyst for specific chemical reactions, converting a specific set of reactants (called substrates) into specific products. Without enzymes, life as we know it would not exist.

Epigenome

Epigenome refers to inheritable traits (over rounds of cell division and sometimes transgenerationally) that do not involve changes to the underlying DNA. Instead, non-genetic factors cause the organism's genes to behave or "express themselves" differently.

Epinephrine

Epinephrine is a catecholamine hormone that is chemically identical to the adrenaline produced by the body, and the names epinephrine and adrenalin are often used interchangeably. When produced naturally by the body, it helps us respond effectively to short-term stress. Epinephrine is also used as a drug to treat asthma attacks, cardiac arrest, and allergic reactions, especially those that could be fatal if left untreated. Epinephrine (adrenaline), norepinephrine, and dopamine are part of the sympathetic nervous system and are known as the "fight or flight" hormones.

Excitotoxins

These are substances, usually amino acids, which react with specialized receptors in the brain in such a way as to lead to the destruction of certain types of brain cells. Glutamate is one of the more commonly known excitotoxins. MSG is the sodium salt of glutamate. This amino acid is a normal neurotransmitter in the brain. In fact, it is the most commonly used neurotransmitter by the brain. How could a substance that is used normally by the brain cause harm? Glutamate, as a neurotransmitter, is used by the brain only in very small concentrations. When the concentration of this transmitter rises above this level the neurons begin to fire abnormally. At higher concentrations, the cells undergo a specialized process of cell death; literally "excited" to death.

Failure to Thrive

Failure to thrive is a description applied to children whose current weight or rate of weight gain is significantly below that of other children of similar age and sex.

Fermented Foods

Fermented foods are foods broken down by the action of microorganisms. Fermented foods contain the beneficial flora

Lactobacillus acidophilus. The bacteria use the starches and sugars in foods as its food. In the process of metabolizing the sugars, the bacteria produce several by-products. The main by-product, lactic acid, actually preserves food because it inhibits other bacteria that cause foods to rot and putrefy. Recent research validates that fermented foods aid in digestion, support immune function, and increase overall nutritional status by adding B vitamins and anti-inflammatory omega-3 fatty acids. Another metabolic by-product of probiotics is a variety of short chain fatty acids that are actually used as a source of fuel by intestinal cells. The combination of keeping the intestinal cells built up and functioning well, the increased nutrients, and the crowding out of pathogenic bacteria help boost our immune system.

Fiber

What we typically think of as fiber is made up of a variety of plant compounds. Plant products contain phytochemicals, which protect first the plants themselves and then the humans who consume them. Whole grains, nuts, seeds, legumes, vegetables, and fruits are all important for a high-fiber diet. There are two main types of fiber: soluble fiber and insoluble fiber. The body needs both to perform different functions. Soluble fiber dissolves in water to form a gel-like substance. It helps the body by absorbing cholesterol and keeping blood sugar levels healthy and the body's energy level balanced. Oatmeal, legumes, barley, and fruits are high in soluble fiber. Insoluble fiber does not dissolve in water. It is not digested but moves through the digestive tract, helping to flush waste out of the digestive system quickly. Whole grains and most vegetables are high in insoluble fiber. Fiber helps keep bowel movements regular and decreases the risk for irritable bowel syndrome and diverticulitis. Fiber can reduce the risk for colon cancer and heart disease.

Food Allergy

A true food allergy is an immune system reaction that occurs shortly after eating an offending food. "Food allergy" refers to a particular type of response of the immune system in which the body produces what is called an allergic, or IgE, antibody to a food. (IgE, or immunoglobulin E, is a type of protein that works against a specific food.) Even a tiny amount of the allergy-causing food can trigger digestive problems, hives, or swollen airways. For some people, the allergy may be life threatening.

Food Hypersensitivities or Intolerances

Food intolerance or non-allergic food hypersensitivity is a delayed, negative reaction to a food, beverage, or food additive involving the IgG immune response. It can involve symptoms in one or more body organs and systems. Food intolerance has been associated with irritable bowel syndrome and inflammatory bowel disease, chronic constipation, chronic hepatitis C infection, eczema, NSAID intolerance, respiratory and ear, nose, and throat complaints, headaches, indigestion, and heartburn. Triggers may range from genetic predispositions, to a viral infection or illness, to environmental chemical exposure. A deficiency in digestive enzymes can also cause some types of food intolerances, including gluten and casein.

Free Radicals

Free radicals are molecules that are not positively or negatively charged, they are usually highly reactive and unstable, and look to bond with other molecules, destroying the host molecule's vigor and setting off a detrimental process within that molecule. Free radicals are responsible for aging, tissue damage, and contribute to the manifestation of some diseases. Antioxidants present in some foods can minimize the impact of free radicals and help prevent damage to healthy tissue.

Glucose

Glucose is used as an energy source in most organisms, from bacteria to humans. Carbohydrates are the human body's key source of energy. Breakdown of carbohydrates yields mono and disaccharides, most of which is glucose. Glucose is taken up by the body in the intestines and distributed to the cells through the bloodstream; where it is further broken down to create the energy for all cellular functions. Glucose is stored primarily in the liver and muscles as glycogen.

Glutathione

Glutathione is a small protein composed of three amino acids: cysteine, glutamic acid, and glycine. Glutathione exists in almost every cell of the body. The presence of glutathione is required to maintain the normal function of the immune system. It is the master anti-oxidant of the body that aids in free radical scavenging, immune boosting, and detoxification of the body. Glutathione is an essential component of your cells, with low glutathione levels; cells cannot perform many of their functions properly.

Gluten

Gluten is found in wheat, rye, and barley grains. Gluten is also used as a stabilizing agent in products like ice cream and ketchup, as well as many other processed and manufactured foods. Gluten is a protein, meaning that it is a chain made from nineteen different amino acids and an imino acid. The chain is quite long, and because of the shapes and electrical charges of the amino acid molecules, and also because of the way the amino acids are connected (called a peptide bond), the chain likes to coil and fold, forming structures that are held together by the attraction of charges on the "outside" of the amino acid molecules. The gluten protein can also occur in short peptide chain fragments (7 - 20 amino acids) from the original protein. The fragments are characterized by the presence of more than one "proline" (one of the twenty amino acids) near another one in the chain. Proline causes there to be a kink in the peptide chain, and human digestive enzymes can't grip it properly to take the chain apart, so intact peptide chain fragments remain. This allows peptide connected sequences to pass through the small intestinal wall where they can meet immune system cells or even be absorbed to circulate in the bloodstream. It is the immune response to the proline-containing peptides that cause many people trouble with gluten. The fragments of the gluten protein trigger an immune system response of the same type that fights off infections.

GMO

Genetically modified organisms (GMOs) can be defined as organisms in which the genetic material (DNA) has been altered in a way that does not occur naturally. It allows selected individual genes to be transferred from one organism into another, also between non-related species. Genetically modified (GM) foods are developed and marketed because there is some perceived advantage either to the producer or consumer of these foods. The initial objective for developing plants based on GM organisms was to improve crop protection. The GM crops currently on the market are mainly aimed at an increased level of crop protection through the introduction of resistance against plant diseases caused by insects or viruses or through increased tolerance towards herbicides.

Heavy Metals

Heavy metals are individual metals and metallic compounds that negatively affect people's health. In very small amounts, some of these metals are necessary to support life. However, in larger amounts, they become toxic. They may build up in biological systems and become a significant health hazard. Examples of heavy metals include mercury, chromium, cadmium, arsenic, and lead.

Heirloom

An heirloom plant is a cultivar that was commonly grown during earlier periods in human history, but which is not used in modern large-scale agriculture. Many heirloom vegetables have kept their traits through open pollination, while fruit varieties such as apples have been propagated over the centuries through grafts and cuttings. Organic heirloom plants can offer superior nutritional value when grown in organic, enzyme-rich soil.

Hormones

Hormones are the chemical messengers in the body. They carry messages from glands to cells to maintain chemical levels in the bloodstream to achieve homeostasis (a state of inner balance between the body's systems and its environment.) The word "hormone" comes from a word that means, "to spur on." Hormones act as a catalyst for other chemical changes at the cellular level necessary for growth, development, and energy.

IgG Food Sensitivities

IgG antibodies are associated with delayed "non-atopic" food reactions that can worsen or contribute to many different health problems. These reactions, also called food intolerances, are more difficult to notice since they can occur hours or even days after consumption of the offending food. Often the offending foods are foods frequently eaten and hard to avoid such as milk, corn, and wheat. IgG food sensitivities are commonly associated with leaky gut and immune system dysfunction.

Immune System

The immune system protects the body from potentially harmful substances by recognizing and responding to antigens. Antigens are molecules (usually proteins) on the surface of cells, viruses, fungi, or bacteria. Nonliving substances such as toxins, chemicals, drugs, and foreign particles (such as a splinter) can also be antigens. The immune system recognizes and destroys substances that contain these antigens. Even your own body cells have proteins that are antigens. Your immune system learns to see these antigens as normal and does not usually react against them.

The organs of the immune system include the bone marrow, Thymus gland, spleen, and lymph nodes. The immune system includes specialized types of white blood cells, known as lymphocytes, produced in the bone marrow. It also includes chemicals and proteins in the blood, such as antibodies, complement proteins, and interferon. Some of these directly attack foreign substances in the body, and others work together to help the immune system cells. Lymphocytes include B cells and T cells. The major function of B-lymphocytes is the production of antibodies in response to foreign proteins of bacteria, viruses, and tumor cells. Antibodies attach to a specific antigen and make it easier for the immune cells to destroy the antigen. The main function of the T helper cell is to augment immune responses by the secretion of specialized factors that activate other white blood cells to fight off infection. They also release chemicals, known as interleukins, which control the entire immune response. Another group of white blood cells is collectively referred to as granulocytes or polymorphonuclear leukocytes (PMNs). These cells are predominantly important in the removal of bacteria and parasites from the body. They engulf these foreign bodies and degrade them using their powerful enzymes.

As lymphocytes develop, they normally learn to tell the difference between your own body tissues and substances that are not normally found in your body. Once B cells and T cells are formed, a few of those cells will multiply and provide "memory" for the immune system. This allows the immune system to respond faster and more efficiently the next time you are exposed to the same antigen, and in many cases will prevent you from getting sick. Immune system disorders occur when the immune response is inappropriate, excessive, or lacking.

Insulin

Insulin is a naturally occurring hormone secreted by the pancreas in response to the presence of glucose molecules in the bloodstream (blood sugar). Insulin binds to the glucose molecules and attaches to an insulin receptor on a cell wall, allowing the cell to absorb the glucose and use it to produce the energy it needs to carry out its function. Without insulin, the cells cannot absorb or use the glucose as energy. In Type 1 diabetes, the body can no longer make insulin because the immune system attacks and destroys the insulin producing cells in the pancreas.

Krebs Cycle

The Krebs cycle refers to a complex series of chemical reactions in all cells that utilize oxygen as part of their respiration process. The Krebs cycle produces carbon dioxide and a compound rich in energy, Adenosine triphosphate (ATP). This chemical provides cells with the energy required for the synthesis of proteins from amino acids and the replication of deoxyribonucleic acid (DNA).

Large Intestine

The large intestine (or large bowel) is the part of the digestive system where waste products from the food you eat are collected and processed into feces. The large intestine is about 5' long and consists of the caecum, appendix, colon, and rectum. The large intestine reabsorbs water and maintains the fluid balance in the body. It absorbs certain vitamins, processes undigested material like fiber, and stores waste before it is eliminated.

Leaky Gut

Leaky gut is the result of damage to the intestinal lining caused by antibiotics, certain drugs, toxins, poor diet, parasites, or infection, making it less able to protect the internal environment as well as to filter needed nutrients and other biological substances. As a consequence, some bacteria and their toxins, incompletely digested proteins and fats, and waste not normally absorbed may "leak" out of the intestines into the bloodstream. Leaky gut is a possible starting point or connection with many disorders such as asthma, diabetes, autoimmune disorders like lupus, scleroderma, internal colitis, rheumatoid arthritis, and can lead to severe illness such as multiple sclerosis, chronic fatigue syndrome, and Crohn's disease. Leaky gut is also linked to the incidence of autism.

Malabsorption

Malabsorption is difficulty digesting or absorbing nutrients from food. Symptoms include bloating, cramping, gas, bulky or fatty stools, chronic diarrhea, muscle wasting, and weight loss.

Methylation

Methylation is not just one specific reaction. There are hundreds of "methylation" reactions in the body. Methylation is simply the adding or removal of a methyl group to a compound or other element. Important methylation reactions include the pairing of methyl groups with toxins so they can be excreted or neutralized by the body, or getting methyl groups to "turn on" serotonin, and thus melatonin production. Methylation is dependant on many factors some of which are the direct availability of nutritional cofactors like vitamin B6, B12, and folate. Low levels of these cofactors along with other nutrients can inhibit methylation, which affects many other metabolic cycles.

Minerals

There two kinds of minerals: macrominerals and trace minerals. The macrominerals group is made up of calcium, phosphorus, magnesium, sodium, potassium, chloride, and sulfur. Trace minerals include iron, manganese, copper, iodine, zinc, cobalt, fluoride, and selenium.

Mineral	What the mineral does	Significant food sources
Sodium	Maintains fluid and electrolyte balance, supports muscle contraction, and nerve impulse transmissions	Sea salt, seaweed, celery, meats
Chloride	Maintains fluid and electrolyte balance, aids in digestion	Sea salt, eggs, meats, goat milk
Potassium	Maintains fluid and electrolyte balance, cell integrity, muscle contractions, and nerve impulse transmission	Green leafy vegetables, mushrooms, avocado, figs, dates
Calcium	Formation of bones and teeth, supports blood clotting	Sesame seeds, green leafy vegetables, sardines, broccoli, oranges

Mineral	What the mineral does	Significant food sources
Phosphorus	Formation of cells, bones, and teeth, maintains acid-base balance	Meats
Magnesium	Supports bone mineralization, protein building, muscular contraction, nerve impulse transmission, immunity	Green leafy vegetables, pumpkin seeds, navy beans, pinto beans, black-eyed peas, sunflower seeds, cashews, halibut
Iron	Part of the protein hemoglobin (carries oxygen throughout body's cells)	Artichoke, parsley, spinach, broccoli, green beans, clams, shrimp, beef liver
Zinc	A part of many enzymes, involved in production of genetic material and proteins, transports vitamin A, taste perception, wound healing, sperm production, and the normal development of the fetus	Spinach, broccoli, green peas, green beans, lentils, oysters, shrimp, crab, turkey (dark meat), beef, lamb, plain yogurt, pumpkin seeds, sesame seeds
Selenium	Antioxidant. Works with vitamin E to protect body from oxidation	Mushrooms, seafood, meats, grains
Iodine	Component of thyroid hormones that help regulate growth, development, and metabolic rate	Kelp, yogurt, eggs, strawberries, cheese

Mineral	What the mineral does	Significant food sources
Copper	Necessary for the absorption and utilization of iron, supports formation of hemoglobin, and several enzymes	Nuts, avocado, lentils, broccoli, mushrooms, oats, seafood
Manganese	Facilitates many cell processes	Green leafy vegetables, pineapple, raspberries, garlic, whole grains
Chromium	Associated with insulin and is required for the release of energy from glucose	Romaine lettuce, onions, tomatoes, liver, whole grains, mushrooms
Molybdenum	Facilitates many cell processes	Beef liver, legumes, dark green leafy vegetables, peas

Mitochondria

Mitochondria provide the energy a cell needs to move, divide, produce secretory products, contract; in short, they are the power centers of the cell. They are about the size of bacteria but may have different shapes depending on the cell type. Mitochondria are membrane-bound organelles, and like the nucleus have a double membrane. The outer membrane is fairly smooth. But the inner membrane is highly convoluted, forming folds called cristae. The cristae greatly increase the inner membrane's surface area. It is on these cristae that food (sugar) is combined with oxygen to produce ATP—the primary energy source for the cell.

Neuron

A neuron is a nerve cell that is the basic building block of the nervous system. Neurons are specialized to transmit information throughout the body. These highly specialized nerve cells are responsible for communicating information in both chemical and electrical forms. There are also several different types of neurons responsible for different tasks in the human body. Sensory neurons carry information from the sensory receptor cells throughout the body to the brain. Motor neurons transmit information from the brain to the muscles of the body. Interneurons are responsible for communicating information between different neurons in the body.

Neurotransmitters

Neurotransmitters are molecular or chemical messengers in the nervous system that transmit information within the brain and from the brain to all parts of the body. Stored in the nerve cell's axon, they relay, amplify, and modulate electrical impulses between one neuron and another through the synapses. There are over 300 neurotransmitters, including serotonin, dopamine, norepinephrine, and acetycholine.

Norepinephrine

Norepinephrine is found in both the central and sympathetic nervous systems, and is produced in the adrenal gland. Besides acting as a neurotransmitter, a chemical responsible for moving nerve impulses between neurons, norepinephrine also acts like a stress hormone. It plays a role in the "fight or flight" response, working in conjunction with epinephrine. When released in times of stress, it increases the heart rate and blood flow to the muscles; it also stimulates the release of blood sugar. Norepinephrine is used to treat dangerously low blood pressure or potentially fatal cardiac-related heart problems.

Nutrition

Nutrition encompasses the broad spectrum of the food materials necessary for cells and organisms to support life. There are six major classes of nutrients: carbohydrates, fats, minerals, protein, vitamin, and water. These nutrient classes can be categorized as either macronutrients (needed in relatively large amounts) or micronutrients (needed in smaller quantities). The macronutrients are carbohydrates, fats, fiber, proteins, and water. The micronutrients are minerals and vitamins. Most foods contain a mix of some or all of the nutrient classes, together with other substances, including toxins. Some nutrients can be stored internally (e.g., the fat soluble vitamins), while others are required more or less continuously. Poor health can be caused by a lack of required nutrients or, in extreme cases, too much of a required nutrient.

Olfactory

The olfactory system is the sensory system used for olfaction, or the sense of smell.

Opioid Effect

Opioid peptides are short sequences of amino acids that bind to opioid receptors in the brain; opiates and opioids (narcotic pain medication) mimic the effect of these peptides. Opioid peptides may be produced by the body itself, for example endorphins, or be absorbed from partially digested food. Three known food substances that can trigger the opioid effect in the body are Casomorphin (from milk), and exorphin and Gliadorphin/gluteomorphin from gluten. The effect of these peptides vary, but they all resemble opiates and can produce "opioid behaviors" when ingested.

Organic

In its most elemental form, the word "organic" means a chemical compound that contains carbon or something that relates to an organ. Organic foods are defined as those that are produced without the use of chemicals, including pesticides and fertilizers commonly used in cultivation, and drugs, such as antibiotics and hormones, given to commercial livestock. Further, foods are held to be organic when the methods of production encourage environmental health and avoid environmentally damaging and destructive actions.

Pancreas

The pancreas makes pancreatic juices and hormones, including insulin. The pancreatic juices are enzymes that help digest food in the small intestine. Insulin controls the amount of sugar in the blood. As pancreatic juices are made, they flow into the main pancreatic duct. This duct joins the common bile duct, which connects the pancreas to the liver and the gallbladder. The common bile duct, which carries bile (a fluid that helps digest fat), connects to the small intestine near the stomach. The pancreas is thus a compound gland. It is "compound" in the sense that it is composed of both exocrine and endocrine tissues. The exocrine function of the pancreas involves the synthesis and secretion of pancreatic juices. The endocrine function resides in the million or so cellular islands (the islets of Langerhans) embedded between the exocrine units of the pancreas. Beta cells of the islands secrete insulin, which helps control carbohydrate metabolism.

Alpha cells of the islets secrete glucagon that counters the action of insulin.

PCBs

PCBs belong to a broad family of man-made organic chemicals known as chlorinated hydrocarbons. PCBs were domestically manufactured from 1929 until they were banned in 1979. Due to their non-flammability, chemical stability, high boiling point, and electrical insulating properties, PCBs were used in hundreds of industrial and commercial applications. PCBs can enter human cells and tissues when contaminated air is breathed in, when contaminated food enters the digestive system, or through contact with the skin. Once in the gastrointestinal tract, ingested PCBs diffuse across cell membranes and enter blood vessels and the lymphatic system. PCBs tend to accumulate in fat-rich tissues such as the liver, brain, and skin. In mothers, PCBs have also been found to pass into the placenta, umbilical cord blood, and breast milk. PCBs can undergo different transformations in the body and then either be stored in certain tissues or excreted. Nonetheless, the evidence suggests that exposure to PCBs is associated with an increased risk of certain cancers of the digestive tract, liver and skin, reproductive deficiencies, neurological problems, and issues with the immune system.

Peptide

A peptide is a compound consisting of two or more amino acids linked in a chain through peptide bonds. Peptide chains consist of 50 or fewer amino acids—proteins are made of multiple peptides.

Phytates

Phytates are salts or esters of phytic acid, the principal storage form of phosphorus in many plant tissues, especially bran and seeds.

Protease

Proteases occur naturally in all organisms. These enzymes are involved in a multitude of physiological reactions from simple digestion of food proteins to a highly regulated cascade (e.g., the blood-clotting cascade.) Peptidases can either break specific peptide bonds, depending on the amino acid sequence of a protein, or break down a complete peptide to amino acids. The activity can be a destructive change, abolishing a protein's function or digesting it to its principal components; it can be an activation of a function, or it can be a signal in a signaling pathway.

Protein

Every cell in the human body contains protein. It is a major part of the skin, muscles, organs, and glands. Protein is also found in all body fluids, except bile and urine. Protein-containing foods are grouped as either complete or incomplete proteins. Complete proteins contain all nine essential amino acids. Complete proteins are found in animal foods such as meat, fish, poultry, eggs, milk, and milk products such as yogurt and cheese. Incomplete proteins lack one or more of the essential amino acids. Sources of incomplete protein include beans, peas, nuts, seeds, and grain. A small amount of incomplete protein is also found in vegetables. Plant proteins can be combined to provide all of the essential amino acids and form a complete protein. An example of a combined, complete plant protein is rice and beans.

Radical Scavengers

One of a group of molecules that combines with free radicals in a chemical or biochemical system to render them less active chemically.

Sensory System

The sensory system is the part of the nervous system responsible for processing sensory information: vision, hearing, somatic sensation [touch], taste, and olfaction [smell]. The sensory system consists of sensory receptors, neural pathways, and parts of the brain involved in sensory perception.

Serotonin

Serotonin acts as a neurotransmitter, a type of chemical that helps relay signals from one area of the brain to another. Although serotonin is manufactured in the brain, where it performs its primary functions, some 90% of our serotonin supply is found in the digestive tract and in blood platelets. Because of the widespread distribution of its cells, it is believed to influence a variety of psychological and other body functions. Of the approximately 40 million brain cells, most are influenced either directly or indirectly by serotonin. This includes brain cells related to mood, sexual desire and function, appetite, sleep, memory and learning, temperature regulation, and some social behavior. In terms of our body function, serotonin can also affect the functioning of our cardiovascular system, muscles, and various elements in the endocrine system.

Small Intestine

The small intestine is the longest portion of the digestive tract, approximately 20' long, and is located within the middle of the abdomen. It has three sections, the duodenum, jejunum and ileum. Much of the small intestine is coiled and suspended in a thin layer of fat; which gives the intestine a lot of flexibility and mobility. Large food molecules are broken down into small molecules that can be transported across the epithelium (lining of the intestinal wall.)

By the time the ingested food reaches the small intestine, foodstuffs have been mechanically broken down and reduced to a liquid by mastication (chewing) and grinding in the stomach. Once within the small intestine, these macromolecular aggregates are exposed to pancreatic enzymes and bile, which enables digestion to molecules capable or almost capable of being absorbed. The final stages of digestion occur on the surface of the small intestinal epithelium.

The net effect of passage through the small intestine is absorption of most of the water and electrolytes (sodium, chloride, potassium) and essentially all dietary organic molecules (including glucose, amino acids, and fatty acids). Through these activities, the small intestine not only provides nutrients to the body, but also plays a critical role in water and acid-base balance.

Synaptic Junctions

The synaptic junction is the region surrounding the point of contact between two neurons or between a neuron and an effector organ, across which nerve impulses are transmitted through the action of a neurotransmitter, such as acetylcholine or norepinephrine. When an impulse reaches the terminal point of one neuron, it causes the release of the neurotransmitter. The neurotransmitter diffuses across the synaptic gap between the two cells to bind with receptors in the other neuron, muscle, or gland, triggering electric changes that either inhibit or continue the transmission of the impulse.

T-Helper Cells

T-helper cells belong to a sub-group of lymphocytes (white blood cells) that provide help to other cells in the immune system by recognizing foreign antigens (a molecule like a bacteria or virus that binds to an antibody) and secreting substances called cytokines (small proteins that affect the interaction and communication between cells) that activate T and B lymphocyte cells. T-helper cells fall into two main classes: those that activate other T cells to achieve cellular inflammatory responses, and those that drive B cells to produce antibodies in what is called the humoral immune response. These two classes of response are generally incompatible with one another and require coordination by substances called cytokines to balance the activation of one type of response while dampening the other. The immune system, when properly activated, works like a teeter-totter between the two types of responses.

T-Helper Cytokines

These cells have a number of different functions, but they get their name from the help they provide to B cells and CTLs (cytoxic T lymphocytes that kill target cells including virus or bacteria infected cells, transplant cells, or cancer cells.) The secretion of the T-Helper Cytokines help stimulate the B and CTL cells and help regulate the body's response to disease and infection.

Thimerasol

Thimerasol is a mercury-based preservative containing ethyl mercury that has been used for decades in the United States in multi-dose vials (vials containing more than one dose) of some vaccines, including influenza vaccines, to prevent the growth of microorganisms such as bacteria or fungi that could contaminate the vaccine. Since 2001, all routinely recommended vaccines (except for the flu vaccine) for administration to young children in the U.S. contain no thimerasol or only trace amounts.

Thymus Gland

The Thymus gland, a specialized gland of the immune system, is located in the upper thorax behind the sternum (breastbone), but below the thyroid gland. The main function of the thymus gland is in the processing and maturation of special lymphocytes called T-cells. The thymus gland is most active during early life, playing a critical role in the development of a child's immune system before birth; usually by the age of two, the thymus gland has reached its maximum size with the immune system becoming fully functional.

Toxins

Toxin is a general term for poisonous substances produced by living cells or organisms or anything that is foreign or poisonous to the body. Toxins can be man-made or may occur naturally in the environment.

Villi

The villi are microscopic finger-like projections that line the inner wall of the small intestine. After food passes from the stomach into the small intestine, nutrients in the food are absorbed into the body through the villi. Every person has millions of villi in their intestines.

Vitamins

Unlike protein, carbohydrates, and fats, vitamins do not yield usable energy when broken down. They assist the enzymes that release energy, but they do not provide energy themselves.

Vitamin	What the vitamin does	Significant food sources
B1 (thiamin)	Supports energy metabolism and nerve function	Green leafy vegetables, mushrooms, tuna, sunflower seeds
B2 (riboflavin)	Supports energy metabolism, normal vision, and skin health	Green leafy vegetables, mushrooms, liver, eggs, berries
B3 (niacin)	Supports energy metabolism, skin health, nervous system, and digestive system	Seafood, beef, poultry, mushrooms, squash
Biotin	Energy metabolism, fat synthesis, amino acid metabolism, glycogen synthesis	Peanuts, all nuts, swiss chard, goat's milk, yogurt, eggs
B5 (pantothenic acid)	Supports energy metabolism	Beef, eggs, nuts, vegetables
B6 (pyridoxine)	Amino acid and fatty acid metabolism, red blood cell production	Spinach, bell peppers, garlic, tomatoes, squash

Vitamin	What the vitamin does	Significant food sources
Folate	Supports DNA synthesis and new cell formation	Green leafy vegetables, liver, lentils, legumes, papaya
B12	Used in new cell synthesis, helps break down fatty acids and amino acids, supports nerve cell maintenance	Meats, poultry, fish, shellfish, milk, eggs
Vitamin C (ascorbic acid)	Collagen synthesis, amino acid metabolism, helps iron absorption, immunity, antioxidant	Green leafy vegetables, berries, citrus, bell peppers, parsley
Vitamin A (retinol)	Supports vision, skin, bone and tooth growth, immunity, and reproduction	Mango, broccoli, butternut squash, carrots, spinach, parsley, sweet potatoes, pumpkin seeds, beef liver
Vitamin D	Promotes bone mineralization	Sunlight, seafood, eggs, liver, fatty fish
Vitamin E	Antioxidant, regulation of oxidation reactions, supports cell membrane and stabilization	Green leafy vegetables, sunflower seeds, olives, almonds, blueberries
Vitamin K	Synthesis of blood-clotting proteins, regulates blood calcium	Avocado, leafy green vegetables, broccoli, cabbage, liver

Betsy and Dr. John Hicks

Betsy and her husband, Dr. John Hicks, bring over 50 years of integrative medical, nutritional, emotional, and vibrational energy experience to their work as speakers, authors, teachers, and healers in the health and wellness community.

Betsy's healing journey began when her son Joey was diagnosed as severely autistic when just two years old. Forced to turn outside the medical community for answers, she became an expert in nutrition and alternative healing therapies. Betsy's book, *"Picky Eating Solutions: Bringing the Joy of Real Food Back to the Table"* gives parents creative and practical solutions to picky eating, and helps them understand the relationship between food and health. A gifted and passionate speaker, Betsy weaves her life experiences and training into a powerful message of creative intention and unlimited possibilities.

From his years of experience in working with chronic illness, Dr. Hicks understands the powerful role that buried emotions and negative thought patterns and beliefs play in the creation of disease. By creating customized biomedical treatment plans for each patient, coupled with the power of thought and Law of Attraction, Dr. Hicks shows his patients how they can unlock their own healing potential. As a team, Betsy and Dr. Hicks are well known in the autism community for their powerful message of love and acceptance, and that message is beautifully demonstrated in Dr. Hicks's forthcoming book about his work with the children of autism and his relationship with his step-son Joey.

In addition to Elementals Living, their health and wellness center, Betsy and Dr. Hicks speak and teach at nationwide conferences, seminars, and workshops, as well as keynote their own series of Elementals Living conferences and retreats.